Healthy

KINGDOM CHURCHES

Healthy

KINGDOM CHURCHES

Ten Qualities of Healthy Churches

PROPERTY OF
PASTOR MICHAEL
WILKES

J. ROBERT WHITE

Published in the United States by Baxter Press, Friendswood, Texas.
Cover design by John Gilmore, Gilmore Marketing, Houston, Texas.
Formatted by Anne McLaughlin, Blue Lake Design, Dickinson, Texas.

ISBN: 1-888237-43-0

The versions of the Bible used in this book are the New American Standard Bible and the King James Version.

Scripture quotations marked KJV are taken from The Holy Bible, Authorized King James Version (Nashville: Holman Bible Publishers, 1987).

Scripture quotations marked NASB are taken from the New American Standard Bible® ©Copyright 1960, 1962, 1963, 1968, 1971, 1972, 1973, 1975, 1977, 1995 by The Lockman Foundation. Used by Permission.

TABLE OF CONTENTS

Dedicated to the memory of my father, J. R. White, a great man of God, a Southern Baptist pastor, and a loving dad at whose feet I learned much about the gifts of pastoral ministry and Gospel preaching. Dad talked for years about writing a book, but never did until now, for his influence upon my love for the church and ministry is reflected throughout this writing.

ACKNOWLEDGMENTS

I wish to express appreciation for my beloved wife, Janice, who has been a constant source of encouragement to me from the first conversation we had about my writing this book. She is, without a doubt, the finest and most consistent Christian I have ever known. We are both grateful to God for our three precious daughters and their husbands, Kathy and Kevin Curtin, Karen and Stephen Lillard, and Jennifer and Aaron Millage. Our girls have been exemplary preacher's kids throughout their lives. They never complained about Dad using them as illustrations in sermons, and I trust they will feel the same about my having used them as illustrations in this book. Through their families, God is blessing us with grandchildren, and we could not be more blessed or thrilled. I have been wonderfully blessed with a family that loves the Lord and His church.

Being born into the home of a Southern Baptist pastor and wife who loved the Lord and the church profoundly has been an immeasurable gift to my life. My parents, J.R. and Nell White, nurtured my two sisters and me in such a wonderful Christian home environment that the most natural decision in all of life for us was to trust

Jesus Christ as Savior and Lord. My father's pastoral gifts continue to influence my ministry on a daily basis.

This book began over lunch in a local restaurant with my two assistant executive directors, Mike Williams and Bobby Boswell. They challenged me to identify the qualities of a healthy church for our Strategy Development Team. I accepted the challenge, and this book is the product of a process that began that day at lunch. No one has ever had two finer Christian visionaries to work with than I have in Mike and Bobby.

From the initial presentation to the Strategy Development Team and then the entire staff, I have received tremendous encouragement from our Convention staff in attempting this project. I am so grateful to our staff for their encouraging me to write this book. I am confident that I would never have attempted it without their words of encouragement. On our staff are three wonderful Christian women with whom I work closely every day, Fran Waymack, Debbie Gaines, and Jeanne Houston. In many ways, this book is a product of their efforts to give me the quiet time necessary to write the book. They have answered many questions I have asked including research issues. Working with these wonderful ladies everyday is a delight.

Fran Waymack, my executive assistant, is the one person without whom this book would never have been published. She has employed her unique literary gifts in the careful reading and editing of the manuscript. Her wonderful sense of humor and attention to details has made the entire process enjoyable. She has spent hours upon hours in communication with the publisher and others in order to see that every detail has been attended to. My special thanks goes to her husband, Parvin, who has encouraged her throughout the editing of this book even though some of that work was done at home on personal time.

Special thanks goes to Dr. Frank Cox, my pastor, who wrote the Foreword for this book. Frank is not only the finest expository preacher I know, he is a true friend. Being members at North Metro First Baptist Church in Lawrenceville, Georgia, has been one of the richest blessings of ministry in Atlanta for my family and me.

I am grateful for my friends, Morris Chapman, Carlisle Driggers, Nelson Price, and Bob Reccord, who agreed to record their thoughts about this book on the back cover. Their friendship over the years has blessed my life immeasurably. Their words have encouraged me, and their ministries have inspired me.

A word of special thanks goes to Pat Springle and Baxter Press. From our first contact with their company, they have been wonderful to work with.

A project of this magnitude is the result of the efforts of many people. I am thankful for each one, and most especially for the Lord, Who has guided me throughout the writing of this book.

J. Robert White

FOREWORD

Recently, I took my children to see a show in Panama City Beach, Florida, featuring a well-publicized Elvis impersonator. I have been an Elvis fan from my youth up and saw him in concert at least eight times when he was alive. I was excited to take my children to share something with them that I had enjoyed so much. The music started, and the show was well on its way. The impersonator, while not Elvis, was doing a pretty good job of imitating the king.

After about five songs, it hit me. This man had the outfit, the dark hair, the moves, and a voice akin to the king, but the problem was, he was not the king. With all the trappings, he was just an imitation of the "real deal." Today, our lives are encroached upon by those who try their best to look like experts in their field, but upon close examination, you will discover they are nothing more than an imitation of the real thing.

When I take time to read a book on healthy Kingdom churches, I want to be certain that the one writing knows what he is talking about. I believe the writer should know his subject scripturally, theoretically, and experientially. When I served as president of the Georgia Baptist

Convention, I was able to observe Dr. J. Robert White up close and had the opportunity to capture a sense of his heart. For the past several years, we have enjoyed a unique relationship as I have served him and his wife, Janice, as their pastor. Believe me, he knows what it takes to build a healthy Kingdom church.

The insight one finds in this book is for the modern day church. Its message is for everyone who desires their church to make a real difference in what some would term a post-Christian era. Bob White writes from his vast experience as senior pastor of growing dynamic churches and his ten years as executive director of the Georgia Baptist Convention. Throughout his ministry as a pastor, he has been about the business of building healthy Kingdom churches. Senior pastors should read this book with a note pad nearby to record the gems of practical wisdom from a Kingdom builder. Pastors of any size church will be encouraged, uplifted, motivated, and inspired by what they read. The key to a healthy church always begins in the heart of the leader, the undershepherd.

However, the sole responsibility of the health of the church must not be confined to the pastor or staff. Healthy churches must be facilitated through faithful servants of God — the lay people. Bob White, through the message of this book, challenges them to greater obedience as they live out their Christian calling. Lay people will discover through *Healthy Kingdom Churches* the church at its practical best, and they will be encouraged by the potential partnership role that they can have in their churches.

Bob White is no imitator. He is the real deal. He has built a life of ministry upon the principles outlined in this book. His passion for the church to impact her world with the Gospel of Jesus Christ will leap from the pages. In these tumultuous, changing times where the standards for growing churches are changing as quickly as they are established, there are Biblical standards that are constant. Read on and allow an experienced developer of healthy Kingdom churches to lay out for you God's blueprint for healthy churches.

Frank Cox
Senior Pastor
North Metro First Baptist Church
Lawrenceville, Georgia

MY HEART IS FULL

few years ago the Georgia Baptist Convention, which I serve as executive director, underwent a restructuring process. There were numerous reasons for the changes that were ushered in. With strict delineation between the various departments of the Convention, the organization was suffering from a serious case of "turfism." There were more layers of management than were necessary to get the work accomplished, and we were not as effective as we needed to be in providing support to our churches and associations. The result of the transformation was a flatter organization with one less layer of management. We became more team-oriented and less cloistered in our departments. We added a second assistant executive director so that one assistant executive director would function in the oversight of business administration and the other in the area of ministry.

A significant piece of the new structure was the addition of nine ministry resource consultants who serve the needs of churches and associations regionally throughout the state. This is significant since Georgia is the largest state in land area east of the Mississippi, and while one half of the population is concentrated in the metropolitan Atlanta area, persons living in other regions of the state often felt disconnected from the Convention. It was our desire to come closer and more personally in touch with the needs of our constituents. Though the new system is not perfect, we are seeing positive signs among our churches and associations and a greater sense of contributing to the whole by our staff.

The Convention's Strategy Development Team (SDT) works consistently to develop strategies which will more effectively equip our staff to assist our churches and associations in becoming all they believe God has called them to be. In the SDT process, my two assistant executive directors, Mike Williams and Bobby Boswell, asked me to prepare a presentation for the SDT on the subject of "Healthy Churches." They specifically asked me to identify the qualities of a healthy church. I laughingly responded, "No way am I going to let you put me in that position." I knew that we had a functioning Church Health Team that had been working on isolating these qualities for some time. They insisted that I make an effort to meet the challenge. Reluctantly, I agreed.

Defining the qualities of a healthy church can be a slippery slope since we believe in the autonomy of the local congregation.

Defining the qualities of a healthy church can be a slippery slope since we believe in the autonomy of the local congregation. What may be the qualities of a healthy church to me may not be the qualities of a healthy church to another. In the preparation of my assignment, I sought to base my opinion upon the Scripture and upon 56 years of experience in the church. I am 56, so how can I claim 56 years of experience in the church? Easy question – I'm a preacher's kid. I have been going to church since before I was born. I can remember being in the preschool nursery at Main Street Baptist Church in Jacksonville, Florida. I remember snack time which usually consisted of two Ritz crackers and a Lily Cup of water. I remember those early years well. They were happy years.

I was one of those kids who loved church. I never resented church as some preacher's children do. My father was pastor of some very fine churches. Our family was always treated well, and the congregation generally pampered us children. I never had a sense that our family was being treated with anything but respect. There were, of course, a few renegade folks along the way who made their presence known, but since my father pastored large churches, these persons were fairly well lost in the numbers of more positively oriented people.

When I was eight years old, I gave my life to Jesus Christ. It happened in Lexington, Kentucky, at the beginning of the summer of 1954. I was so moved by the Spirit of God while our family worshiped with my grandparents at Immanuel Baptist Church that I wanted to go forward at the invitation time. I held myself back since this was not my home church, and I had not yet spoken to my parents about my desire to trust Christ as my Savior. For some time, I had been aware that I was unprepared for death. Every night at bedtime, I prayed the child's prayer: "Now I lay me down to sleep. I pray

Thee, Lord, my soul to keep. If I should die before I wake, I pray Thee, Lord, my soul to take." Some in our current day reject the idea of a child praying a prayer like that, which focuses a child's mind upon death. In my life, God used that prayer to convict me of my need to be saved. You might say, "That's not good. Fear is not a good motivation to come to Christ." Did fear have anything to do with my deciding that I needed a personal relationship with Jesus Christ? It certainly did, and it was a healthy fear, if I might say so. Fear is not necessarily a bad thing. Certainly the wise parent will teach his child to fear a hot stove or the danger of cars passing on the street. One evening after I had prayed that prayer, I lay in my bed with my eyes and heart wide open. I realized that I needed Jesus. I had reached what we commonly refer to as "the age of accountability." Across the years my knowledge of the Lord and His love for me has grown as has also my personal commitment to Him.

That Sunday afternoon in June 1954, I talked with my parents about what I had felt in my heart at church that morning. As we sat on the sun porch of my grandparents' home, I prayed for God to forgive me for the sins of my life. I invited Jesus Christ to come into my heart. At that very moment, God saved me by His grace. He gave me the gift of eternal life, a gift that I desperately needed but did not deserve. From that day forward my love for the Lord has grown, and He has been far better to me than I deserve. My sins have been

I invited Jesus Christ to come into my heart. At that very moment, God saved me by His grace.

forgiven—all of my sins. I have been cleansed of those sins by the blood of Jesus shed on the cross for me and for you. It is the miracle of God. To be sure, it is a miracle of transformation, spiritual healing, and cleansing from sin that can happen no other way.

While in college at Samford University in Birmingham, Alabama, I felt God's call to enter the ministry. When I publicly dedicated my life to the ministry, numerous persons at my home church, First Baptist Church of Montgomery, Alabama, said, "We are not surprised. We have known for a long time that God was calling you into the ministry." I thought that was strange since this was a matter that I had struggled with for a couple of years and had difficulty discerning God's will for my life. It was wonderfully reassuring and confirmed for me that I was indeed following God's will for my life.

I pursued my theological education at The Southern Baptist Theological Seminary in Louisville, Kentucky. While there, I was called to serve as pastor of my first church, Dabney Baptist Church in Holton, Indiana. It was a wonderful, friendly, and supportive congregation, just what I needed in my first years as a pastor. My wife, Janice, and I have talked many times about how lovingly they listened to many bad sermons and then made me feel that I was the greatest preacher in all the world as they encouraged me.

I remember Pop Tucker as a great encourager. In the winter, he always got to the church early to see that the heater was working and the church was warm when people began to arrive. He sat to my left under the large wall clock with its long pendulum that made that beautiful homey tick tock sound throughout the worship service. One cold, snowy Sunday evening, Pop Tucker was the only one who showed up for church besides Janice and me. The roads were treacherously icy, and I really wanted to close up for the night and start the long 80-mile drive back to the campus in Louisville. Gingerly I asked, "Well, what do you think I ought to do?" Pop Tucker said, "About what?" "What do you think I ought to do about the worship service tonight?" He replied with conviction, "I came to worship. I want to hear your message." That night Janice filled in at the piano. The three of us sang the hymns. Then I preached as though the church house was filled to capacity.

On another occasion, Pop Tucker said, "Pastor, I suppose you see me writing throughout your message every Sunday. I want you to know that I am paying attention. I am making notes from your sermon. Then, all week long while I am out on my tractor on the farm, I pull those notes out of my pocket, and I read them over and over. You will never know how much I get out of your sermon as I review your message throughout the week. You are helping me a lot through your preaching, and I want to thank you." What a wonderful gift that was to a young pastor who needed to be encouraged and needed to be reminded that every trip to the pulpit requires serious preparation for the preaching of God's Word.

After seminary, I served as associate pastor to my father at the First Baptist Church of Montgomery, Alabama. What a delightful experience that was as this man whom I knew as "Dad" shared with me from the depths of his 40 years in pastoral ministry. What I learned in those two and one-half years was an incredible complement to my years of formal seminary education as I applied what I learned in the classroom in the laboratory of real church life.

From the wonderfully nurturing experience of First Baptist Montgomery, I was called to Tabernacle Baptist Church in Carrollton, Georgia, where I served as pastor for over seven years, then to the First Baptist Church of Paducah, Kentucky, where I served as pastor for eleven years. Both of these churches were strong churches with memberships of 2,400 and 3,300, respectively. During those 18 years, God nurtured me and trained me for the opportunity I now have to minister among the 3,500 churches of the Georgia Baptist Convention. In my position, I have been able to preach in small churches and large churches, in rural areas and major cities, from north to south, from east to west. I

I have seen healthy churches and unhealthy churches.

have been intentionally observant of the similarities and differences in churches. I have seen healthy churches and unhealthy churches. I have witnessed organized, visionary pastors and pastors who are laid back and just take it as it comes.

Frankly, I can say that I have loved the church all of my life. I am devoted to the church and to its success in the most challenging days and culture, perhaps, in the history of the world. The qualities of healthy Kingdom churches that I have brought together in this book are assembled from personal experience and observation over the course of my lifetime. This is not intended to be a book of scientific research on the theme of healthy churches, nor is it exhaustive of the subject. It is intentionally written from my heart and my background of growing up in the home of a pastor, serving as a minister in churches for 25 years and as executive director of a state convention of churches for ten years. Writing from the perspective of experience and observation will result in a more subjective than objective outcome. This, however, is

My heart is full, and I need to share what I am feeling deep within.

what I have dreamed of doing across the years. My heart is full, and I need to share what I am feeling deep within. You are certainly free to disagree with my list of ten qualities of Healthy Kingdom Churches. I am strongly convicted about these ten, however, and I expect that, while the list is not exhaustive, many will agree with the necessity of these ten qualities.

As we approach the discussion of these ten qualities, let us remember that Jesus established the church to be healthy so that its mission might be accomplished. In Matthew 16:13-18 KJV, it reads, "When Jesus came into the coasts of Caesarea Philippi, he asked his disciples, saying, Whom do men say that I the Son of man am? And they said, Some say that thou art John the Baptist; some, Elijah; and others Jeremiah, or one of the prophets. He said unto them, But whom say ye that I am? And Simon Peter answered and said, Thou art the Christ, the Son of the living God. And Jesus answered and said unto him, Blessed art thou, Simon Barjona: for flesh and blood hath not revealed it unto thee, but my Father which is in heaven. And I say also unto thee, That thou art Peter, and upon this rock I will build my church; and the gates of hell shall not prevail against it."

Stuart K. Weber, in the *Holman New Testament Commentary, Matthew,* says that the Roman Catholic Church has erroneously used this text to provide the basis for its doctrine of Peter being appointed as the first in a long line of Popes. He proceeds to say that also in error are Protestants who have gone to the other extreme, allowing the word "rock" to apply to anything but Peter himself. Weber asserts that Jesus is clearly saying that Peter and the other disciples with their understanding of Christ's identity will be the "living stones" of the church (1 Peter 2:5). It was upon the understanding of Peter's confession that the church would be built. Christ was saying that Peter would be the first spokesman among those who would become the custodians of the truth about Jesus' identity. We remember from Peter's sermon in the early pages of Acts how powerfully Peter declared the truth about Jesus' identity.[1]

Notice that when Jesus spoke of the church, He referred to it as "My church."

Notice that when Jesus spoke of the church, He referred to it as "My church." The name of Christ, His character, His person, and His principles are to be represented by the church. Jesus said that the gates of hell would not prevail against His church. The gates of a city were a symbol of that city's strength. Jesus was saying,

---

1 Stuart K. Weber, *Holman New Testament Commentary, Matthew* (Nashville, Tennessee: Broadman & Holman Publishers, 2000), pp. 250-251.

It is the vision of Christ for His church that its health and its resulting strength would be such that the evil in the world would not be able to overcome it.

"My church is unstoppable. Satan cannot corral it. Nothing can overpower or silence my community of faith, not even the power of death itself. My church will go on, even if its individual members should die."[2]

Clearly, Jesus was envisioning a healthy church that would prevail in a lost world. It would confront every stronghold of Satan and come out the victor every time. I love that! It is the vision of Christ for His church that its health and its resulting strength would be such that the evil in the world would not be able to overcome it. The church would work diligently to bring the Kingdom of God on earth. The church would seek to build the Kingdom of God, not its own kingdom.

The Apostle Paul speaks of the healthy church in an unhealthy world in another way. He writes, "I beseech you therefore, brethren, by the mercies of God, that ye present your bodies a living sacrifice, holy, acceptable unto God, which is your reasonable service. And be not conformed to this world, but be ye transformed by the renewing of your mind, that ye may prove what is that good, and acceptable and perfect will of God" (Romans 12:1-2 KJV). In the succeeding verses of that chapter of Romans, Paul gives his own list of qualities of a healthy church:

"For through the grace given to me I say to every man among you not to think more highly of

---

2 Ibid., p.252.

24

himself than he ought to think; but to think so as to have sound judgment, as God has allotted to each a measure of faith. For just as we have many members in one body and all the members do not have the same function, so we, who are many, are one body in Christ, and individually members one of another. And since we have gifts that differ according to the grace given to us, let each exercise them accordingly: if prophecy, according to the proportion of his faith; if service, in his serving; or he who teaches, in his teaching; or he who exhorts, in his exhortation; he who gives, with liberality; he who leads, with diligence; he who shows mercy, with cheerfulness. Let love be without hypocrisy. Abhor what is evil; cling to what is good. Be devoted to one another in brotherly love; give preference to one another in honor; not lagging behind in diligence, fervent in spirit, serving the Lord; rejoicing in hope, persevering in tribulation, devoted to prayer, contributing to the needs of the saints, practicing hospitality. Bless those who persecute you; bless and curse not. Rejoice with those who rejoice, and weep with those who weep. Be of the same mind toward one another; do not be haughty in mind, but associate with the lowly, do not be wise in your own estimation. Never pay back evil for evil to anyone. Respect what is right in the sight of all men. If possible, so far as it depends on you, be at peace with all men. Never take your own revenge, beloved, but leave room for the wrath of God, for it is written, 'Vengeance

is Mine, I will repay, says the Lord. But if your enemy is hungry, feed him, and if he is thirsty, give him a drink; for in so doing you will heap burning coals upon his head.' Do not be overcome by evil, but overcome evil with good."
(Romans 12:3-21 NASB)

While there are many qualities of a healthy church, I will list ten.

QUALITY #1:
PREACH AND TEACH
THE GOSPEL OF CHRIST

*I*t was June 17, 1873, when the great evangelist, Dwight L. Moody, and his song leader, Ira D. Sankey, landed on the shores of Liverpool, England. They had gone there on a mission of great faith. Moody said that it was his prayer that they would see 10,000 people come to faith in Jesus Christ during the revival effort. D.L. Moody said that he was praying that the revival fires would begin to flicker in Great Britain, then jump across the Atlantic, and a great, God-sent revival would come to America. Then Dwight L. Moody prayed this prayer, "Dear Lord, if this revival spirit in me ever dies, may I die with it." What a great prayer that was. I have often wondered how many of us would be willing to pray a prayer like that.

What was Moody saying in that prayer? I think he was saying, "Lord, if I can look upon the world and see people who are lost without Christ and have no compassion for

Life will not be worth living if I can't live it as a Christian who is on fire for Christ.

their spiritual condition, just take me on home. Life will not be worth living if I can't live it as a Christian who is on fire for Christ. If I can see people wondering aimlessly like sheep without a shepherd and have no concern about their dying lost without Jesus Christ, I'd rather die. I don't want to live as a lukewarm Christian." Would you be willing to make a statement like that? Could you pray a prayer like that?

There is no substitute for the preaching and teaching of the Gospel of Christ. Now, I am certainly aware that our culture has become much too sophisticated to believe that there is only one way to receive eternal life. The politically correct thing to say is that there are many ways to go to heaven when you die. Many people today accept the religion of self-righteousness. "I will go to heaven when I die because I am good. It is inconceivable to me that God would send a good person to hell. I am a faithful husband, a faithful father. I work hard to earn an honest wage. I pay my taxes. I've never intentionally hurt any-one. I've never stolen anything or killed anyone. I am a good person. Surely you would not say that God would prevent me from going to heaven."

Actually, God will not prevent anyone from going to heaven. God wants everyone to have eternal life. You are the only one who can prevent you from going to heaven. God does not send people to hell. People send themselves to hell by rejecting God's plan of salvation. This truth could not have been more clearly stated than Jesus said it in His own words:

"For God so loved the world, that he gave his only begotten Son, That whosoever believeth in him should not perish, but have everlasting life. For God sent not his Son into the world to condemn

the world; but that the world through him might be saved. He that believeth on him is not condemned: but he that believeth not is condemned already, because he hath not believed in the name of the only begotten Son of God. And this is the condemnation, that light is come into the world, and men loved darkness rather than light, because their deeds were evil."
(John 3:16-19 KJV)

I remember a few years ago, on an early Sunday morning, hearing Dr. James Kennedy preaching on television. Dr. Kennedy is an evangelistic Presbyterian preacher and senior pastor of the Coral Ridge Presbyterian Church in Fort Lauderdale, Florida. He was preaching on this very subject. As I recall, he put it this way, "Many of you have been asking me for years: 'Why do bad things happen to good people?' Now there is a book that has been published that bears that very title, *Why Do Bad Things Happen To Good People?* I want to answer that question for you today. Why do bad things happen to good people? The answer, of course, is because there are no good people. The Bible says in Romans 3:10 KJV, 'As it is written, There is none righteous, no, not one.'" Paul used the words, "As it is written…" Where else might this be found? In Psalm 14:3 KJV, the Psalmist declares, "They are all gone aside, they are all together become filthy: there is none that doeth good, no, not one." Clearly, the Bible teaches that even one sin separates us from God. One sin in a lifetime is enough to eternally separate us from the holy and perfect God. Most of us would be honest enough to say that we are guilty of far more than one sin. One sinful thought, word or action is sufficient to condemn us to eternal separation from God.

So, what is the answer? Jesus is the answer! God, in His love for us, sent Jesus to this world to pay our sin debt by giving His life on the cross. Jesus, Who was perfect in every way and did not deserve to die, took the place of all of us who most certainly deserve to die because of our sin. Then God, Who is sovereign and therefore has the right to decide how people will be saved from their sins and receive the gift of eternal life, instructed us that the only way to be forgiven from our sins and receive His gift of eternal life is to believe in His Son, Jesus Christ. Acts 4:12 NASB states this truth so clearly that even a child can understand it: "And there is salvation in no one else; for there is no other name under heaven that has been given among men, by which we must be saved." It is through faith in Christ, and Christ alone, and receiving Christ, and Christ alone, that we are saved. It is this act of receiving that transforms a person from being a lost sinner to being a saved sinner. The miracle of salvation happens when a person who believes that Jesus is the Christ, the Son of God, then invites Jesus into his or her life.

It is through faith in Christ, and Christ alone, and receiving Christ, and Christ alone, that we are saved.

Belief is essential to salvation, but so is receiving. John 1:12 KJV points this out clearly: "But as many as received him, to them gave he the power to become the sons of God, even to them that believe on his name." There have been many lost people who believed that Jesus is the Son of God, the Savior of the world, yet never invited Christ into their hearts and, therefore, never experienced salvation. Simply put, if you offer a gift to me, but I fail to reach out my hand and receive it, it's not my gift. It becomes my gift when I receive it, when I express appreciation and accept that which is being offered to me. It is this same way with salvation. Christ, through His death on the cross, is extending a wonderful gift to you. It is the gift of forgiveness and the gift of eternal life. Will that gift become yours? It's up to you.

Why aren't there other ways to receive eternal life? There are no other ways to receive eternal life because God said this is the way to be saved. Nothing else will do except that we trust Jesus Christ as Savior. God can establish the rules because He is God, and God can do it any way He wants to. You may argue with that. You may disagree with it. You may even stomp your foot and declare that you don't like it. Nothing is changed by negative reactions to the greatest truth the world has ever received.

In John 14:1-6 NASB, Jesus is discussing with His disciples the subject of eternal life in heaven. Thomas responded to Jesus' discourse by saying, "Lord, we do not know where You are going; how do we know the way?" Jesus said to him, 'I am the way, and the truth, and the life; no one comes to the Father, but through Me.'"

Universalism, which is not taught in the Bible, declares that eventually everybody will be saved. The idea is that, after a person dies, there will be other opportunities to trust Jesus Christ as Savior and be saved. That may have a "good feel" for folks who would like to live life singing Frank Sinatra's song, "I Did It My Way." There is, however, no Biblical evidence that life can be lived without Christ, then conveniently, in one's own time after death, make a commitment to Christ and be saved.

Those who have received Christ will be welcomed into heaven but those who have rejected Him will be eternally lost.

Actually, what the Bible teaches is this: "And as it is appointed unto men once to die, but after this the judgment" (Hebrews 9:27 KJV). After death comes the time of judgment when those who have received Jesus as Savior and those who have rejected Him will be separated into two groups. Jesus clearly addresses this event in Matthew 25:31-46 NASB.

Those who have received Christ will be welcomed into heaven but those who have rejected Him will be eternally lost.

"But when the Son of Man comes in His glory, and all the angels with Him, then He will sit on His glorious throne. And all the nations will be gathered before Him; and He will separate them from one another, as the shepherd separates the sheep from the goats; and He will put the sheep on His right, and the goats on the left. Then the King will say to those on His right, 'Come, you who are blessed of My Father, inherit the Kingdom prepared for you from the foundation of the world. For I was hungry, and you gave Me something to eat; I was thirsty, and you gave Me drink; I was a stranger, and you invited Me in;

naked, and you clothed Me; I was sick, and you visited Me; I was in prison, and you came to Me.' Then the righteous will answer Him, saying, 'Lord, when did we see You hungry, and feed You, or thirsty, and give You drink? And when did we see You a stranger, and invite You in, or naked, and cloth You? And when did we see You sick, or in prison, and come to You?' And the King will answer and say to them, 'Truly I say to you, to the extent that you did it to one of these brothers of Mine, even the least of them, you did it to Me.' Then He will also say to those on His left 'Depart from Me, accursed ones, into the eternal fire which has been prepared for the devil and his angels; for I was hungry, and you gave Me nothing to eat; I was thirsty, and you gave Me nothing to drink; I was a stranger, and you did not invite Me in; naked, and you did not clothe Me; sick, and in prison, and you did not visit Me.' Then they themselves also will answer, saying, 'Lord, when did we see You hungry, or thirsty, or a stranger, or naked, or sick, or in prison, and did not take care of You?' Then He will answer them, saying, 'Truly I say to you, to the extent that you did not do it to one of the least of these, you did not do it to Me.' And these will go away into eternal punishment, but the righteous into eternal life."

The fire that Dwight L. Moody felt burning within should be felt by all of us once we understand that the only way to heaven is through faith in Christ. The only way we would not have that fire within would be if, first, we do not believe that Jesus is the only way, and second, we don't care if people are lost. Neither of these two options is acceptable so our response should be to preach and teach the Gospel of Christ with all of our hearts and energies until life on earth for us is ended. I'll join D.L. Moody in his commitment. I want to be a preacher who is on fire for Christ.

I want to be a preacher who is on fire for Christ.

While serving as pastor in another city, a good friend of mine was also serving as pastor in a nearby church. My friend had a wonderful personality, so when he appeared at my office door on a Monday morning with a big smile on his face, I expected to hear something funny. He did not disappoint me. He told me about a wedding they had at his church on Saturday evening. He said that everything was beautiful. There were flowers and candles everywhere. The ladies were dressed in long beautiful dresses and the men in black tuxedos. The pastor told me that he was wearing his long black pulpit robe which he always wore for formal weddings.

He said that everything was going well in the ceremony until they reached the time for the wedding vows. At that point he said that he noticed the groom lost all the color from his face. He began to wobble and weave. My friend began to think about what he might do if the groom passed out. He had heard of other ministers having this problem, but for him it was a first-time experience.

Just then, the mother of the groom who was seated on the second pew jumped up and ran up onto the platform. She knew her boy better than anyone else, and she knew he was getting ready to faint. My friend told me that she threw her arms around her boy to give him support. You can imagine how confusing this must have been in the midst of a formal wedding. My friend told me that she was a rather large woman which complicated the situation. He said, "I backed up to get out of the way and didn't realize it, but I backed into the candles that were behind me. My robe burst into flames and the organist cried out, 'Preacher, you're on fire!' The groomsmen jumped on me, pushed me to the floor and rolled me over and over till the fire was out."

> **"My robe burst into flames and the organist cried out, 'Preacher, you're on fire!'"**

Overwhelmed by this story I asked, "What did you do then?" He said, "Well, my robe was still smoldering, but I guess all the excitement helped the groom to recover. He seemed fine so I finished the ceremony with my robe still smoking." "That's not all," he continued. "Sunday morning when I came to the pulpit, I said to the congregation, 'You all have been saying for years that you wanted me to be a preacher who was on fire. Well, now I have had that experience, and I want you to know I'm prepared for it.' At that point, I unbuttoned my coat and revealed that I had hung a fire extinguisher over my belt."

I want to be a preacher on fire for Christ. Don't you want to be a Christian who is on fire for Jesus? What about your church? Don't you want people to say of your church that they have never seen a church so much on fire for Christ? What a great statement to be made about a Christian or about a church.

One night while I was serving as pastor of the First Baptist Church of Paducah, Kentucky, as I was at home eating dinner with my family, the phone rang. It was Fletcher Schrock. Fletcher was a young attorney in our community and his wife Bonnie was the news anchorwoman on the NBC affiliate in our city. This was one of the finest couples in our church. Fletcher was volunteering for the evening at our recreation building. When I answered the phone, Fletcher was obviously excited. "Bob, I think there is a fire somewhere in the church building. The alarms are going off. I have looked around the Christian Outreach Center, but I can't find a fire anywhere." I assured Fletcher that I would be there shortly. In a matter of minutes I was in the utility room at the church checking the fire alarm system. I was able to successfully reset the alarm, which was a good indication that there was not a real fire. A power surge, or some other cause, had set off the alarm.

I went back to the recreation building to inform Fletcher that everything was fine. He said, "Something funny just happened. Bonnie called from the television station to say that she had heard over the police scanner that there was a fire at First Baptist Church." Then I remembered that our alarm system was tied directly to the police and fire stations. Just then I heard the sirens coming. I ran out into the street beside the church in time to see the fire engines, the fire chief, the police chief, and the reporter from the T.V. station all pulling up to the church at the same time. I was embarrassed as I ran toward them waving my arms and announcing in a loud voice, "Our church is not on fire! Our church is not on fire!" As I drove home that evening those words played over and over again in my mind, "Our church is not on fire. Our church is not on fire." Then I prayed, "Lord, please don't let it be said of our church that we are not on fire." Now, obviously, I didn't want a fire in our church, but

> **Then I prayed, "Lord, please don't let it be said of our church that we are not on fire."**

I did want our church to be known as a church that was on fire for Jesus Christ! Don't you want your church to have that reputation?

The Apostle Paul had started the church at Thessalonica in the midst of great persecution. From Thessalonica he traveled to Berea, Athens, and then Corinth. I am sure that he frequently wondered how the new church at Thessalonica was doing under the oppression of persecution. When he learned that they were thriving, truly a church on fire for Christ, he commended them for the wonderful qualities of a church that was on fire for Christ. An outstanding quality mentioned by Paul is found in 1 Thessalonians 1:8 NASB, "For the word of the Lord has sounded forth from you, not only in Macedonia and Achaia, but also in every place your faith toward God has gone forth, so that we have no need to say anything."

Paul commended them for preaching the Gospel of Christ. They had been faithfully sounding forth the word of the Lord, day by day, and week after week, until people were hearing far and wide about the great revival God was sending to Thessalonica.

The Greek verb in that verse has the connotation of a trumpet blast or the roll of thunder. I prefer to think of the second since I am from the South where we hear lots of thunder. We are to be reminded that our churches are to thunder the Gospel of Christ so that, like thunder, it rolls out across the countryside declaring the good news about God's love expressed through Jesus Christ, God's Son.

I had been at my new church in Kentucky for just a few weeks when someone asked me, "Pastor, did the search committee tell you that we are in tornado alley here in Paducah?" When I asked what that meant he said, "Well, what it means is that all the tornados that come up the Ohio River Valley pretty much come right through our city." Then I thought, "Isn't it amazing what search committees don't tell you about the church and the area before you come?" I decided not to tell my wife about this, because I didn't want her to worry about it. When that first big thunderstorm of the season came up, it was about 2 A.M. one morning. The lightning was popping and the thunder was rattling the windows. You could hear the thunder rolling across McCracken County. I sat up in bed to listen for a tornado, but I didn't wake my wife, Janice, who was sleeping soundly. Around 2:30 A.M. I heard a tornado. If I have ever heard anything about a tornado, it is that it sounds like a freight train. I heard it, and I felt it as the house was shaking. I woke Janice up and said, "Honey, there's a tornado over our house. We need to get the girls and go downstairs. Do you hear it? It sounds like a freight train." She sat up in bed and listened and agreed that it did sound like a freight train. Just then it went "Woo-woo. Woo-woo." It was a freight train! I forgot that the railroad tracks were just a couple of blocks from our house.

The next time a thunderstorm approaches your home, listen to the storm. Think about what you are hearing. Hopefully, you will not hear a tornado. As you listen to the thunder rolling across the countryside, think about this verse, and remember that a sure sign of a church that is alive and healthy, a church that is on fire for Christ, is that it is thundering the Gospel of Jesus Christ.

Not long ago I preached the Sunday morning worship service in a Georgia church. I preached a message about the cross of Christ. At the end of the service, I was informed by the associational missionary that there were two deacons in the worship service from a neighboring church. These men wanted to talk with me about their church. They were concerned because their church was dealing with some serious controversy within the congregation. The two men approached me. The one who began to speak had tears in his eyes. "Dr. White, I want you to know that your sermon this morning is the first sermon I have heard on the cross of Christ for, I don't know how long. Our pastor does not preach the Gospel." I asked, "What does he preach, if he doesn't preach the Gospel?" The deacon replied, "Well, last Sunday he preached about fat people." Giving the pastor the benefit of the doubt, I assumed by that statement that possibly he had preached on the body as the temple of the Holy Spirit and how we are to keep our temple fit. The deacon told me that mostly they hear messages that you might hear at some civic function, usually about social issues.

I was certainly deeply concerned about the health of the church the deacons described that day. I was also troubled over the fact that this was not the first time I had heard this remark. Numerous others have said to me at various times, "Dr. White, you would be amazed to know how few pastors are really preaching the Gospel." There is apparently a dearth of preaching about Jesus. What have we to preach if we don't preach the Gospel? There is no other message for the church to declare.

> **What have we to preach if we don't preach the Gospel?**

The world needs to hear a word from God. Like the eighth century prophets, we should stand and boldly declare, "Thus saith the Lord God of Hosts...."

When I was pastor of the Tabernacle Baptist Church in Carrollton, I usually went up to the church on Saturday afternoon to check through the sanctuary in order to make sure that everything was clean and straight for Sunday morning. I had an excellent staff to take care of those sorts of things, but I just wanted to know that we were ready for Sunday. One Saturday afternoon, in the process of walking throughout the sanctuary, I sat down in the balcony on the front row. I know the Lord led me to that place for He spoke to me in a way that I have never forgotten. I looked over the edge of the balcony at all the empty pews below. Our sanctuary seated about 1,200 people. I looked at all of those seats, and while I was looking, God spoke to me. It was not an audible voice, but

I knew it was God. He said, "Look at all of those empty pews. Tomorrow morning they will be filled with men and women, young people, boys and girls who have come to receive a word from God. Are you ready? You know how long it takes for you and Janice to get your three daughters ready for church. Many of these families have young children. They have to go through a lot in order to get ready and get the family to church. Will they be disappointed, or will you feed my sheep?" Getting Kathy, Karen, and Jennifer ready for church when they were little girls was a process that began on Saturday night. There were white shoes to be polished; hair had to be washed and rolled; baths had to be given; dresses had to be ironed. It was quite a process. Then on Sunday morning it was often quite a hassle to get everyone up, dressed and to church in time for Sunday School. Since we had early worship services, Janice had to take all of the Sunday morning duty by herself. It's not easy getting all of the family ready and to church on Sunday, but it is vitally important to do so. It is also vitally important that, when people arrive at the church on Sunday morning, they find good food for their souls. The pastor, church staff, and the Sunday School leadership should feel a great weight of responsibility not to disappoint those who come to worship. They need to hear a word from the Lord.

When I was ordained to the Gospel ministry in 1968, I sat before an ordination council at my home church, First Baptist Church of Montgomery, Alabama. This was a seasoned group of Baptist ministers and Christian laymen. It was a wonderful time that we shared together that Sunday afternoon. Many words of advice were given to me. The wise counsel that I remember most came from my father who said, "Always be certain to faithfully preach the Word of God. There are more good sermons in the Bible than could be preached in many lifetimes. You will never exhaust the Bible. If you ever base your sermons upon anything but the Bible, you will be in trouble. If you preach the Bible and base your ministry upon God's Word, you will always be upon firm footing."

"... If you ever base your sermons upon anything but the Bible, you will be in trouble."

Since my father was also my pastor, you now know the kind of preaching under which I grew up. I was also blessed by many wonderful lay people in our church who gave of themselves to teach Sunday School and Discipleship Training, or Training Union as it was called when I was a boy. These wonderful people taught me the Word of God faithfully week after week. There is no way to measure their impact upon my life.

I will never forget Mrs. Skinner. She taught me both on Sunday morning and on Sunday evening, Sunday School and Training Union. I loved her. Her life story was truly amazing. Before she became a Christian, she was a bareback rider in the circus. She was the petite young lady who stood on the back of the horse as he went around in the circle performing many stunts. One day she came to know and trust Jesus Christ as her Savior, and her life was changed forever. I did not know her in the earlier years. I saw her much later in life after she had matured in her faith and shared her faith with us boys and girls. She would often make chocolate fudge and give it to the boys and girls who learned their Scripture lessons well, or in the case of Training Union, said their parts well. The Skinners lived out in the country on a farm and frequently would have the young people out to their farm for fishing and cooking out.

I went off to college and then to seminary. Years went by. Then, wonderfully, I was invited back to my home church to serve as an associate pastor with my father. I learned that Mrs. Skinner had contracted cancer. I went to visit her in the hospital. Now I was the minister, ministering to her. It was such a special joy because she had ministered to me as a child and young person. As I stood at her bedside, tears filled my eyes. She must have seen them because she said, "Bobby, don't you worry about me. My life belongs to Jesus. I am ready to go to heaven when He is ready for me." Then she spoke the words of a chorus which we had sung together many times as I grew up in the church:

> **If a church is to be a healthy church there is no substitute for preaching and teaching the Gospel of Christ.**

"Everyday with Jesus is sweeter than the day before.
Everyday with Jesus, I love Him more and more.
Jesus saves and keeps me, and He's the One I'm living for.
Everyday with Jesus is sweeter than the day before."[1]

---

1 Robert C. Loveless and Wendell P. Loveless, "Sweeter Than the Day Before," *The Broadman Hymnal*, ed. B.B. McKinney (Nashville: Broadman Press, 1940), p. 325.

If a church is to be a healthy church there is no substitute for preaching and teaching the Gospel of Christ. Not only is it a quality of church health, it is a quality which produces healthy Christians.

As I shared with my Convention staff the qualities of a healthy church which I am discussing in this book, someone asked, "Do you have these qualities listed in order of importance?" My answer was that they are not in any particular order other than the fact that I do personally believe that the number one quality of a healthy church is "Preaching and Teaching the Gospel of Christ." This quality has no equal. No church can be healthy without it.

🔲

QUALITY #2: WORSHIP THAT INSPIRES

A few years ago the story was reported of a New Mexico woman, Mario Rubio, who was frying tortillas when she noticed that the skillet burns on one of her tortillas resembled the face of Jesus. Excited, she showed it to her husband and her neighbors. They all agreed that there was a face etched on the tortilla and that it bore a remarkable resemblance to Jesus.

The woman went to her priest to have the tortilla blessed. She testified that the tortilla had changed her life, and her husband agreed that she had been a more peaceful, happy and submissive wife since the tortilla had arrived. The priest, who was not accustomed to blessing tortillas, was reluctant but agreed to do it.

The woman took the tortilla home and put it in a glass case with piles of cotton to make it look like it was floating on clouds. She built a special altar for it and opened the little shrine to visitors. Within a few months, more than 8,000 people came to the shrine of Jesus of the tortilla. All of them agreed that the face in the burn marks on the tortilla was the face of Jesus. Everyone agreed except for one reporter who said that he thought it looked more like the former heavy weight boxer champion, Leon Spinks.

It seems incredible that so many people would worship a tortilla, but such a distorted concept of worship is not really that unusual in our culture. It is sad that, though the Bible is clear about how, Whom and when we are to worship, far too little genuine worship takes place.

When our daughter, Karen, was away in college, she went to church one Sunday morning at a large church that was known for its dynamic worship services and evangelistic outreach. She sat down next to a very nice senior adult lady. The lady kept glancing in Karen's direction, then finally asked, "Are you one of those sweet little college students?" Karen replied that she was a college student. "Are you visiting with us today?" Karen replied that she was a visitor. The lady paused for a moment and then with great enthusiasm said, "You are going to love our show!"

"You are going to love our show!"

Karen was shocked, but when I heard about it, I thought it was probably a very honest, and not too uncommon, appraisal of what many people think about their worship service. Now, I like for the worship experience to be exciting, but somehow it needs to stop short of being a "show."

To experience worship that inspires, the pastor needs to assume the responsibility to plan the worship event carefully and in concert with music leadership and others who may be involved in the worship leadership. Too many times I have been in a worship service and heard the preacher say when he went to the pulpit after the special music, "Isn't God amazing! I didn't know what the music was going to be this morning, and the minister of music didn't know what my message was about, but God knew. It just demonstrates the miraculous power of the Lord that He has put this service together as He has with everything fitting together so beautifully." It's wrong to have to expect God to work a miracle every Sunday when the pastor should take the lead in worship planning. There are too many demonstrations of church staff leadership failing to discuss together the most important hours of the week, the hours of worship.

While that planning should stop short of planning a "show," the activity on the platform during the worship service should be well-timed and well-coordinated so as not to be a distraction to the worshipers. Time should be conserved for worship music and the preaching of the Gospel without lengthy time lapses and gaps between those who are coming to the pulpit to speak. The people in your congregation are accustomed to seeing quality communications wherever they go throughout the week. They are used to seeing quality, and when it is not there, they notice. Since worship involves the praise and adoration of God, it deserves nothing less that the very best in planning and execution.

Since worship involves the praise and adoration of God, it deserves nothing less that the very best in planning and execution.

I can give a real example of how thoughtful worship planning might have avoided an embarrassing moment. My dad told me about a revival he preached one time when the pastor of the church announced that it was time to receive an offering for the evangelist.

The pastor went to great lengths to promote the offering for "Brother White," noting what a blessing he had been to the church during the week of revival, and it was only right that the church respond with a generous offering. He then invited the ushers to come forward to receive the special offering. The organist played as her offertory for the evening, "It Pays to Serve Jesus."

Throughout the Bible the importance of worship is emphasized. In the very beginning, in Genesis, the fall of man came when man failed to worship God. In Revelation, it is revealed that all of history culminates in the worship of Almighty God Who is worthy of all praise and glory. Revelation 19:3-6 KJV speaks of the worship of God in heaven:

> "And again they said, Alleluia. And her smoke rose up forever and ever. And the four and twenty elders and the four beasts fell down and worshiped God that sat on the throne, saying, Amen; Alleluia. And a voice came out of the throne, saying, Praise our God all ye his servants, and ye that fear him, both small and great. And I heard as it were the voice of many waters, and as the voice of many thunderings, saying, Alleluia: for the Lord God omnipotent reigneth."

These words remind me of the Hallelujah Chorus: "And He shall reign forever and ever. King of Kings and Lord of Lords, Hallelujah, Hallelujah." What a glorious experience that will be when we gather at the throne of God to worship Him and to sing praises to His name forever and ever.

Jesus referred to the commandment in Deuteronomy 6:4-5 as the greatest commandment: "And Jesus answered him, the first of all the commandments is, Hear, O Israel; The Lord our God is one Lord: and thou shalt love the Lord thy God with all thy heart, and with all thy soul, and with all thy mind, and with all thy strength: this is the first commandment" (Mark 12:29-30 KJV). This word from Jesus is a call to worship which affirms worship as a priority.

The very first of the Ten Commandments regulates worship. In this commandment, God specifies that there is to be no worship of other gods. Jesus also makes this clear in Matthew 4:10 KJV, "Then saith Jesus unto him, Get thee hence, Satan: for it is written, Thou shalt worship the Lord thy God, and him only shalt thou serve."

In the Old Testament, the tabernacle, the place of worship, was central among the Israelites. The centrality of the tabernacle demonstrates the priority upon worship. The tabernacle was designed only for worship. It was the place where God met His people. There were no seats in the tabernacle for the children of Israel did not go there to attend a service or to be entertained. They went to worship God. If they had a meeting for any other purpose than worship, then it took place somewhere else. The tabernacle was in the very center of the camp of Israel. All of the tribes set up camp so that they faced the center, the place of worship.

Throughout the Scripture, worship is central. The fact is, we were made to worship. Everyone worships, even

Everyone worships, even an atheist. He worships himself.

an atheist. He worships himself. When a person rejects God, he takes up the worship of false gods. This, God forbade in the very first commandment: "Thou shalt have no other gods before me" (Exodus 20:3 KJV).

In the New Testament, Jesus spoke of a new day for the worshiper. Jesus said that the time is coming and now is when the worshiper would not be tied to a location. The true worshiper, He said, would worship the Father in spirit and in truth (John 4:23). Then Jesus said, "God is spirit; and those who worship Him must worship in spirit and in truth" (John 4:24 NASB).

The importance of attending corporate worship is clearly expressed in Hebrews 10:25 NASB, "not forsaking our own assembling together, as is the habit of some, but encouraging one another; and all the more, as you see the day drawing near."

I'll never forget as long as I live my visit to the catacombs in Rome. These underground passages where many were buried during times of great persecution against Christians still bear the evidence of worship which took place there nearly 2,000 years ago. Those Christians assembled in these secret places for worship at the risk of losing their lives. Surely, as dangerous as these gatherings were, they provided times of encouragement for believers during terrible days of persecution.

Just as terror drew those early believers together for worship, terror in our day has had an effect upon worship attendance. George Gallup, Jr., reports statistics for "Emerging Trends," a newsletter of the Princeton

Religion Research Center. The newsletter from December 2001 reported on worship attendance following the terrorist attacks of September 11, 2001. The report states: "In the immediate wake of the terrorist attacks, increased numbers reported praying and attending church. A late September Gallup survey, however, showed church attendance returning to pre-September 11 levels."[1]

In America we are blessed with freedom to worship without fears of being prevented from worshipping due to persecution. The real question is why many Christians place such a low priority on worship. Sure, we turn to God in a crisis, but as the immediate crisis subsides, quickly revert to our old ways of relegating the worship experience to a lower priority. The worship service is not just another meeting to attend during the week. Corporate worship of God presents a unique opportunity to experience the divine presence of God. When believers gather for worship, God shows up. The Spirit of God moves among the worshipers to comfort broken hearts, heal hurts and convict lost people of their need for a personal relationship with Jesus Christ. As a pastor, it was not an unusual thing to be approached by someone who would say, "I am so sorry I missed church on last Sunday. If I had known what great things were going to take place, I would have been here." I always wanted to respond, "Well, why weren't you here? Anytime you miss gathering for worship with God's people you miss the miraculous presence of God." We should expect to miss a great blessing whenever we miss church.

---

1 "Emerging Trends." Princeton Religion Research Center, Vol. 23, No. 9, December 2001, p.1.

What do I mean when I speak of worship that inspires? Worship that inspires us to do what? I am of the conviction that the leadership of the church should settle for nothing less than worship services that stir the heart and thrill the soul. Something should happen when worship of God takes place. Lost people should be profoundly convicted of their sins and want to be saved. Believers should desire to confess their sins and live more effectively for Christ. Young people should receive strength to live for Christ in a pagan culture. Believers should be encouraged to be bold witnesses for Christ. Members of the church should gain a vision of what it means to be a missionary at home and across the world. Worship should encourage Christians to get involved in being a missionary where they live, or perhaps, even going across the world as a mission volunteer to make a difference in lives that might otherwise never even hear the name of Jesus. In worship there should be tears, laughter, and chill bumps. Worship should provide experiences that the worshiper will never forget as long as he or she lives. Lives should be deeply impacted and changed forever during the hour of worship.

> **I am of the conviction that the leadership of the church should settle for nothing less than worship services that stir the heart and thrill the soul.**

Every time I think about the witness of worship, I think about Charlie. I met Charlie on a Sunday morning at First Baptist Church in Paducah, Kentucky where I was pastor. Our morning worship services were televised live over WPSD-TV, the local NBC affiliate. I had completed my sermon and was standing at the front to receive those who were responding to the invitation. We were on the final stanza of the invitation hymn when I saw a young man with long dark hair, dressed in jeans and a tee shirt running down the aisle. I went to him, and the first thing he said was, "Is it too late for me to become a Christian?" I responded, "No, it's not too late. You are right on time." He went on to explain, "I was watching your church over television this morning. I came to understand that I needed Jesus in my life. When you finished your sermon I ran out, got on my motorcycle, and got over here as fast as I could. So, I'm not too late?" "No," I assured him, "You are not too late. We are thrilled that you have come today to ask Jesus into your life." We sat on the front pew, and I had the privilege of sharing with him God's wonderful plan of salvation. He prayed to receive Christ. The congregation was thrilled to meet Charlie, a new believer in Christ, and also a testimony to the power of the Gospel presented in the hour of worship. It was a moment that also greatly encouraged our television crew as they saw clear evidence of fruit from their ministry.

A frequently addressed question related to the quality of the worship experience focuses upon the style of worship. There has been no small debate among our churches on the subject of contemporary worship versus traditional worship or blended worship. The Research Services Department of the Georgia Baptist Convention reported in January 2002 its findings related to growth trends among Georgia Baptist congregations from 1995 to 2000 based upon differences in worship style also on whether the church had adopted a written mission, vision or purpose statement. The study revealed that the patterns of difference among the various congregations studied are not determinative. That is, there are declining contemporary style churches and many growing traditional style churches. Church growth cannot be reduced to one or two variables; many factors contribute including demographics, leadership, vision, purpose, organization, etc.[2]

In 1999, churches and mission congregations in the Georgia Baptist Convention were asked two survey-type questions on the Annual Church Profile, one relating to worship style and the other to mission statements. The two questions read as follows:

(1) Check the box that best describes the style of your primary worship service(s). If multiple services, please check all that apply.
Contemporary, Blended, Traditional.

(2) Has your church adopted a written mission, vision or purpose statement within the past 5 years?
Yes, No.

No definitions or examples of worship styles were given in the Annual Church Profile instructions. The churches gave their own self-perceptions of their styles.[3]

---

2 Steve Whitten, "Growth Patterns Among Georgia Baptist Congregations: A Report on Worship Style and Mission Statements, Research Services, Georgia Baptist Convention, January 2002, p.1.

3 Ibid, p.2.

The Executive Summary of the survey contains the following pertinent information:

- About one-third of Georgia Baptist Convention (GBC) congregations have adopted a written mission, vision or purpose statement within the past five years.

- Two-thirds of GBC congregations identify their primary worship style as exclusively traditional.

- More than one-third of reporting GBC congregations (982) indicate they have a service with a contemporary or blended worship style.

- Overall, 64% of GBC congregations were plateaued or declining in resident member growth and growth in average weekly Sunday School attendance from 1995 to 2000; 36% were growing.

- In worship attendance, 44% of GBC congregations were growing from 1995 to 2000.

- From 1995 to 2000, churches that had adopted a written mission, vision or purpose statement outgrew churches that had not adopted such a statement: 41% of churches with mission statements were growing versus 35% of churches without mission statements. Worship attendance growth rates show a similar pattern: 47% of churches with mission statements were growing in worship attendance versus 43% for those without a statement. For average

Each growth measure showed lower rates of declining churches among congregations that had adopted a mission statement.

weekly Sunday School attendance, the figures are 39% growing for mission statement churches compared to 35% for churches without mission statements. Each growth measure showed lower rates of declining churches among congregations that had adopted a mission statement.

- Churches with contemporary or blended worship styles outpaced churches with exclusively traditional worship styles in three indicators of church growth from 1995 to 2000: (1) percent resident member growth (41% growing to 35% growing); (2) percent growth in worship attendance (47% growing to 43% growing); and (3) percent growth in average weekly Sunday School attendance (39% growing to 35% growing). Also, the percentages of churches declining in all three categories were lower for blended and contemporary churches than for traditional only churches.

- A comparison of the three largest worship style response groups (traditional, blended, contemporary) shows that churches with contemporary only worship styles are the fastest growing in worship attendance (52% - more than half - are growing) and resident membership (46% growing). In average Sunday School attendance growth, blended only churches are the fastest growing (40%).

- Congregations with blended or contemporary worship styles have adopted mission, vision or purpose statements at rates significantly higher than churches with exclusively traditional worship styles. Almost one of five (18.5%) traditional worship style churches has adopted a mission, vision or purpose statement. By comparison, more than half of contemporary only churches (57%) and of blended only churches (54%) have adopted a mission statement.

- Contemporary and blended only churches comprise about half of all churches which have adopted a written mission statement, but represent only 31% of responding churches.[4]

It does appear that churches, regardless of the worship style, that have an understanding of who they are and where they are going have clearly demonstrated an appeal that draws more people to worship. Whether contemporary, blended or traditional, there is no substitute for making every effort to reach the unchurched and draw them to a worship experience which is meaningful to them. Worship may vary depending upon the leadership and, in particular, the community in which the church resides. Whatever the location, style of worship or prospective members, every worship service, Sunday morning, Sunday night, Wednesday night, or other, should reflect the joy that we have in Jesus Christ

---

4 Ibid, p.3.

and should have a consistent spiritual appeal that will draw people time and time again to a meaningful and inspiring worship experience.

CHAPTER 3

⬧

QUALITY #3: PRIORITY ON PRAYER

A number of years ago, I had the opportunity to go to Hong Kong on a preaching mission with the International Mission Board. On the way, a group of us stopped off in Taipei, Taiwan. We ate dinner at the hotel with 60 of our missionaries serving in that part of the world. On the next morning, we were taken for a brief tour of the city. One stop was at a Buddhist Temple. It was my first visit to a Buddhist Temple so I was intrigued to see all of the ornate gold statuary, candles, and other trappings. While there, I took time to observe the people who were coming in and out of the temple. I don't suppose I will ever forget a petite, elderly woman who entered, approached the altar, and took some red sticks from a jar. She then started throwing them to the floor. Once she threw them on the floor, she would lean over them for a long while looking at them and then scoop them up and throw them again. This happened repeatedly. Each time I could not help but notice the look of sheer desperation upon her face. Her eyes reflected a deep sadness.

I asked our guide what this was about, and he explained that she was seeking an answer from her god with these sticks. As the sticks fell to the floor, they produced differing patterns which supposedly provided a message to her from her god. The guide said that, as you could see, she was not very happy about the outcome. Apparently, she did not get the response that she was hoping for.

I thought of the words of the Psalmist:

"Their idols are silver and gold, the work of men's hands.
They have mouths, but they speak not:
eyes have they, but they see not:
They have ears, but they hear not:
noses have they, but they smell not:
They have hands, but they handle not:
feet have they, but they walk not:
neither speak they through their throat.
They that make them are like unto them;
so is every one that trusteth in them."
(Psalm 115:4-8 KJV)

I wanted to chase after her and tell her that the answer to her prayers is not to be found in throwing sticks to the floor, but in a personal relationship with Jesus Christ.

I wanted to chase after her and tell her that the answer to her prayers is not to be found in throwing sticks to the floor, but in a personal relationship with Jesus Christ. I wanted so much for her to know that there is a true God Who knows her and loves her, Who will indeed hear and answer her prayers. I wanted her to know that our God has a mouth through which to speak. He has eyes to see with, ears to hear with, and a nose to smell with. He has hands to touch our every need, and feet to walk with us through hard times and good. I cannot communicate adequately to you the deep sense of personal frustration I felt that day as the truth of the Gospel was so close to her, but I had no way to communicate it to her. She had now disappeared among the crowds on the street, and if I could find her, I could not communicate

I opened the Gospel tract and handed it to him.

with her. I have thought about that woman many times over the years. I have prayed that somehow God was able to get the truth communicated to her. I have prayed for the many others like her in the world today, people who are religious, but are spiritually lost because they have not trusted in the only One who can give them salvation.

One day while in Hong Kong, I sat on a park bench for the better part of an afternoon praying for an opportunity to share my faith. I watched the older men and women walking by and the younger children playing. In my hand were spiritual tracts written in Chinese. I couldn't read them, but that wasn't necessary. I understood the message from each page of the tract because of the pictures. The person I would witness to would be able to read the Chinese. I didn't know for sure how all of this would come together, but I know our God is able. Sure enough, after awhile an older gentleman came along and seemed curious about why this American was sitting in the park. I motioned for him to sit down beside me which he did. I opened the Gospel tract and handed it to him.

Together we turned through each page. He read while I pointed at the pictures. At the end of the presentation, I prayed for this man, and he responded by smiling. I watched him as he walked away to see if he would throw the tract in the garbage can that was nearby or take it with him. He slid the tract into his pocket as he walked away. I have prayed for that man for years that God would save him. I know that God is able.

Prayer for the Christian is so much more than throwing red sticks on the floor, but for many it is just about as effective because they hardly ever pray. The real mystery about prayer is not unanswered prayer. The real mystery about prayer is unoffered prayer.

Jesus has given us a wonderful promise in the Sermon on the Mount about God's will to answer our prayers. It is apparent that Jesus is saying that so much more of God's goodness for us would be revealed if we were just faithful to pray. Here is what He said:

> "Ask, and it shall be given to you; seek, and you shall find; knock, and it shall be opened to you. For every one who asks receives, and he who seeks finds, and to him who knocks it shall be opened. Or what man is there among you, when his son shall ask him for a loaf, will give him a stone? Or if he shall ask for a fish, he will not give him a snake, will he? If you then, being evil, know how to give good gifts to your children, how much

Every great church that I have known personally has been a praying church with a real priority on prayer.

62

more shall your Father who is in heaven give what
is good to those who ask Him!"
(Matthew 7:7-11 NASB)

What is true for the individual believer is also true for
the church. The healthy, Kingdom-minded church will
consistently and faithfully ask, seek, and knock in an
effort to know and to do God's will. Every great church
that I have known personally has been a praying church
with a real priority on prayer. Every great revival in
history has begun as a result of concerted prayer on the
part of God's people as they longed to see revival come.

The promise of revival found in 2 Chronicles 7:14 KJV
certainly places a priority on prayer: "If my people, which
are called by my name, shall humble
themselves, and pray, and seek my
face, and turn from their wicked
ways; then will I hear from heaven,
and will forgive their sin, and will
heal their land."

**Revivals are effective
in some churches and
not in others.**

Another great promise of prayer is found in Jeremiah
33:3 KJV: "Call unto me, and I will answer thee, and show
thee great and mighty things, which thou knowest not."

I was at my physician friend's office trying to get well
for an upcoming revival meeting. "You've got to give me
some kind of medicine that will clear up this problem
quickly so I can preach a revival next week. Isn't there
anything that can be done?" He responded, "Oh, I think
we can help you out. You said that you are going to be
preaching a revival next week? I didn't know churches
were still having revivals. Are revivals still effective?" He

was genuine in his query, and I wanted to give him a good response. I said, "Revivals are effective in some churches and not in others." "How do you explain that?" he asked. "Well," I responded, "it's like most other things. The success of a revival is determined largely by the amount of effort that is put into getting ready for revival." He said, "In that case, I hope those folks have put a lot of effort into getting ready for this revival because we are going to do the best we can to have you ready for it."

My doctor friend did get me ready physically for that revival, and I was so thankful that the church also prepared well for the revival. The pastor shared with me at the beginning of the week that they had been praying every day for weeks that God would do something unusual during the revival meeting. He told me that they had been urgently calling upon God through prayer for revival. The church had also been heavily involved for weeks in visiting persons in their city who had visited the church and had shown interest in coming to know Christ. Other prospect names had come in from church members who shared names of relatives and acquaintances who needed Christ.

God did an unusual work that week in revival because the congregation had been praying for weeks that they would see a great revival.

During that wonderful week of revival at Atco Baptist Church in Cartersville, Georgia, where Wayne Hamrick is pastor, we saw 57 people come to faith in Christ. One evening there were over 20 who responded in one service. There were many other decisions as people made commitments of rededication, and others came on transfer of membership. I will forever remember the excitement of the congregation as the aisles filled up with people at invitation time. They got what they prayed for. God did an unusual work that week in revival because the congregation had been praying for weeks that they would see a great revival. Then they put feet and hands to their prayers as they visited throughout the community witnessing to the lost and unchurched.

I couldn't help hearing the words of my doctor friend ringing in my mind, "I didn't know churches were still having revivals. Are revivals still effective?"

Numerous churches, or perhaps I should say pastors, have concluded that revivals are no longer effective. This erroneous evaluation has been made apparently due to weak response to revivals in the past history of either the pastor or the church or both. I would suggest to you that revivals are as effective as they have ever been, but we have failed to pray sufficiently and witness sufficiently to see strong attendance and many decisions for Christ. This is not a matter of cultural change related to our day and time. The revival at Atco was not that long ago. Other great responses to the Gospel of Christ are being registered across the country and the world. People are as hungry for what the Gospel has to offer as they have ever been. God's people simply need to get serious about praying for revival in our time. It's

> **It's wrong to announce the death of revivals in the church when the only reason they may be dead in your church is a lack of commitment to pray for revival and reach lost people for Jesus.**

wrong to announce the death of revivals in the church when the only reason they may be dead in your church is a lack of commitment to pray for revival and reach lost people for Jesus. Revival will not happen without a significant amount of prayer and effort on the part of the entire church and especially the church staff.

A healthy Kingdom church is most certainly one that faithfully prays and lives the words of The Model Prayer, or The Lord's Prayer as it is commonly called. You will recall that one of Jesus' disciples asked Jesus to teach the disciples to pray as John taught his disciples to pray. Jesus instructed them to pray like this: "Our Father Who art in heaven, Hallowed be Thy name. Thy Kingdom come. Thy will be done, On earth as it is in heaven" (Matthew 6:9-10 NASB).

"The Kingdom of God" refers to the reign of God in the universe.

Every congregation would certainly agree about the importance of following the admonitions of The Lord's Prayer, but what does it mean to pray, "Thy Kingdom come. Thy will be done, on earth as it is in heaven"?

"The Kingdom of God" refers to the reign of God in the universe. God's Kingdom existed before time and is in operation today. It will also have a final consummation and perfection. God's Kingdom has application to the individual, God's rule in the heart of the individual person, and to the whole of society, God's rule throughout.[1]

---

1 "Empowering Kingdom Growth: Seeking First the King and His Kingdom," Report of the Empowering Kingdom Growth Task Force. Southern Baptist Convention, St. Louis, Missouri, June 11-12, 2002, p. 2.

In eternity past, Satan rebelled against the Kingdom of God and eventually brought that rebellion to earth inciting man to sin against God. The entire human race was hopelessly implicated and entangled in the rebellion. God's response to Satan's rebellion is the cross of Jesus Christ. Through Jesus, God is redeeming believers one by one, reestablishing His reign on earth in general, and in the hearts of men and women, boys and girls in particular. While the outcome of God's response to Satan is certain triumph, the people of God, the church, must wage spiritual warfare as soldiers of the cross under the command of Christ until "...the end, when He delivers up the Kingdom to the God and Father, when He has abolished all rule and all authority and power. For He must reign until He has put all His enemies under His feet" (1 Corinthians 15:24-25 NASB).[2]

Perhaps you are wondering just how your church should be involved in reclaiming the Kingdom of God on earth. Consider these important questions:

- Do I help my church keep the "big picture" in mind, recognizing the gravity and the urgency of Kingdom business as we plan and execute our ministry?

- Do I encourage my church to recognize our local ministry as part of the larger whole?

- Do I subjugate my own desires in order that the whole body of Christ may be served?

---

2 Ibid., p.2.

- Do I endeavor to maintain the unity of the Spirit in the bond of peace?

- Do I challenge my fellow church members to be salt and light in every arena of their lives, bringing glory to God (Matthew 5:13-16) and growth to the Kingdom?

- Does my church have a heart for the Kingdom of God around the globe?

- Do we pray for the Kingdom to come in all the earth?

- Do we value Kingdom work done by others?

- Do we send resources (personnel, money) to other strategic battlefronts and cooperate with Christian efforts beyond our own locale?[3]

That there is great power in prayer is without dispute. The real question is why we as Christians fail to make prayer a daily priority. Now, I realize that is a generalization, and there are many Christians and many churches that pray fervently and consistently. However, so many would have to give the testimony that it's not that they don't believe in prayer, it's just that they don't think about praying all that much. Oh, there's prayer at mealtime, that is, if we aren't eating out.

That there is great power in prayer is without dispute.

---

3 Ibid., p.3.

It's embarrassing to pray when eating in a public place. Then, of course, there's prayer at bedtime, just before I go to sleep, that is, if I don't fall asleep while I am praying, or begin thinking about other things. It's so easy to get distracted, you know. Did you ever think of prayer in a public place as a part of your witness? Such moments should be reverent and not a boisterous demonstration of spirituality for the entire restaurant to hear. Recently, I was eating out and saw a family of mom and dad and small children bowing their heads and praying quietly before they began their meal. It blessed me and encouraged me to witness their commitment to giving thanks through prayer.

It just may be that if Christians would be more mindful of our witness in the community, it might make a difference in the level of spirituality in the community. That being said, we must always be careful that our prayers are genuine and from the heart. Start early with your children teaching them the importance of prayer. In turn, children often teach us how real prayer is through their openness with God. Don't you just love the innocent straightforward way that children relate to prayer? One evening when our girls were small, Janice went in to hear their prayers. Jennifer, our youngest, had a pretty bad day as I recall. She had been rather disobedient that evening. When Janice heard her prayers at bedtime, Jennifer pretty much rushed through her prayer and quickly said, "Amen." Janice said, "Jennifer, don't you have some things you need to talk to God about tonight?" Jennifer's reply was quick and confident, "No, I don't, but Karen does!"

Wayne and Karen Ramey were members of our church in Kentucky. Their son, Chris, had quite an experience with prayer when he was three years of age. He had been watching "The Incredible Hulk" on television, and as a result, had begun to have nightmares about monsters. On one very frightening occasion he ran screaming to his mother and said, "I had a bad dream. It was a monster, and he was going to eat me!" Karen, speaking softly and trying to calm him down, said, "Oh, Chris, he wasn't going to eat you." "Yes, he was mom. The monster was going to eat me," he insisted. Karen said, "How do you know he was going to eat you?" Chris said, "He was leaning over me and he prayed, 'Thank you, God, for this food.'"

These stories from our children really reflect some of the problems adults have in prayer. Too often our prayers of confession turn into prayers about those other people who have wronged us. At other times, perhaps, the only time we pray is when we are preparing to eat. For many people, prayer is what you do when you have an emergency. Evidence of this attitude about prayer surfaces in the remark, "Well, I guess there is only one thing left to do now— pray." In other words, when the situation is truly hopeless and nothing else seems to be working, then we will resort to prayer. True prayer must be more than crisis management. Even the one most casually related to God will recognize that there is something wrong with going to God in prayer just at times of crisis. True prayer is an ongoing process of

True prayer must be more than crisis management.

drawing near to God where a person does not disassociate prayer life from routine events. This is surely what the Apostle Paul was saying when he said, "Pray without ceasing" (1 Thessalonians 5:17 KJV).

One of the most remarkable prayer experiences I have ever heard was told to me by my father. At the time this story took place, he was pastor of the Cane Run Baptist Church on Iron Works Pike outside of Lexington, Kentucky. This lovely red brick church sits in the middle of the most beautiful horse farms in the Bluegrass. Dad said, "I was into my sermon when there was a clap of thunder, and then rain began hitting the windows. Noah Simpson, one of our fine deacons, stood up right in the middle of my sermon and said, 'Brother White, I hate to interrupt your sermon, but I need to ask the church to pray for my farm. I came to church this morning rather than working on my farm on Sunday, and I have my crop in the fields. If it gets wet, I'll be ruined financially. I want to ask the church to pray that God won't let it rain on my crop.'" At that point Dad said to the congregation, "All of you know Noah Simpson and his family. He is one of our fine deacons and is a faithful tither to the Lord. I think it is appropriate for us to pray that God won't let it rain on Noah's crop."

That morning, during the thunderstorm, the church prayed that God would not let it rain on Noah's fields. Dad said, "After church, when I got home the phone was ringing. I picked it up and heard a very excited Noah Simpson on the other end of the line. He said, 'Preacher, I drove home through mud puddles. It rained all around my farm, but I want you to know that I have been over

71

my entire farm and not a single drop of rain fell on my farm.'"

Now, is that a coincidence or the power of God in response to prayer? There is no doubt. God heard and answered that prayer.

One of the young men in my church made an appointment to talk to me. Jamie arrived at the appointed time and began to pour out his heart. He told me that he loved golf and had always wanted to be golf pro at a golf club somewhere, but his wife thought that would be too risky. He told me that she wanted him to sell insurance. Jamie said that he was convinced that he could be a very effective witness in a golfing environment, and he was feeling God's leadership in that direction. I said, "Jamie, if you feel that God is leading you to pursue this career, and you want to use it as a means of effectively sharing your faith with others, we need to pray about it." We got on our knees and prayed that God would open up a place where Jamie could use his skill as a golf pro and also be a witness for the Lord.

A couple of weeks went by and Jamie came to see me. "You won't believe this when I tell you! God has answered our prayer. I got a call from the Sea Pines Golf Club in Hilton Head, South Carolina. They have asked me to come to work for them as golf pro. I don't even know how they got my name. I am overwhelmed."

Coincidence? Or answered prayer? I have no doubt in my mind that God heard and answered our prayer. I could go on and on with stories of how I have seen God answer prayers directly just as they were prayed. There have been, of course, other prayers that were not answered as they were prayed, but that, too, is a blessing as God knows exactly what we need and what is best for us.

One of the clearest signs that a church is a healthy church is that the church is deeply committed to the power of prayer as it goes about its Kingdom business. We should pray often, "Thy Kingdom come. Thy will be done, on earth as it is in heaven."

One of the clearest signs that a church is a healthy church is that the church is deeply committed to the power of prayer as it goes about its Kingdom business.

CHAPTER 4

QUALITY #4: CONSCIENTIOUS, VISIONARY LEADERSHIP

*O*ne cold day during the Revolutionary War, George Washington was walking among his soldiers in the trenches. He was wearing an overcoat that covered his medals and badges which would otherwise clearly identify him. He noticed a corporal standing to one side of a group of men who were building a wall to fortify their location. The soldiers had been successful in lifting into place all but one huge timber. They were trying with all their might to raise the over-sized log as the corporal shouted encouragement. He was yelling, "Come on, men, you can lift it! Here we go again! Ready, set, push!" The troops were slipping, sliding, and falling in the mud as they attempted to hoist the timber into position. The corporal never offered assistance, but instead, simply repeated the process of barking orders at his men.

Washington observed the situation for a period of time until he could stand it no more. He went over and helped the weary soldiers lift the log and place it on top of the fortification. He still wore his coat which hid the signs of his rank. As he looked over at the corporal he asked, "Why didn't you help your men when they needed you?"

The man replied, "Why, I am a corporal, sir!"

At this statement, Washington unbuttoned his overcoat. "I am the Commander-in-Chief," he said. "The next time your men have a job which they cannot do alone, do not hesitate to call for me. I will be glad to come and help."

Jesus spoke of the proper servant leadership attitude in Matthew 20:25-28 KJV:

"Ye know that the princes of the Gentiles exercise dominion over them, and they that are great exercise authority upon them. But it shall not be so among you: but whosoever will be great among you, let him be your minister; And whosoever will be chief among you, let him be your servant: Even as the Son of man came not to be ministered unto, but to minister, and to give his life a ransom for many."

Jesus was the greatest leader to ever walk on this earth. Remember that He knelt before each of His disciples and washed their feet. Remember that He "...made himself of no reputation, and took upon him the form of a servant, and was made in the likeness of men: And being found in fashion as a man, he humbled himself, and became obedient unto death, even the death of the cross" (Philippians 2:7-8 KJV).

Jesus was the greatest leader to ever walk on this earth.

Being a servant leader is essential for a minister. I would venture to say that the fact that so many never capture this concept explains why in our own state convention in Georgia we are seeing two ministers a week forcibly terminated from their leadership positions. The pastor must not "lord" his position over the staff or the church family. Rather, he must jump down into the muddy trenches to be there with his congregation in their worst days as well as their best days. He must be there for his staff, heavily involved in shouldering the responsibilities with them, not simply barking orders.

We all know what visionary leadership means. I think it is absolutely essential for any effective leader to possess it. A friend, Bill Taylor, director of Network Partnerships for Lifeway Church Resources, shared with me that visionary leadership means having the ability to see what you

Great leaders lead by example.

want to see before you see it. He went on to say that if you can't see it before you see it, you will never see it. A visionary is a person who can see with great clarity and reality his dreams for the future. He is able to project a future outcome in his mind, thus creating a visible mental target. Having seen his dream, he leads others to come along with him on the journey of making the dream a reality. Bringing people along with him is where the visionary leader distinguishes himself. Great leaders lead by example. They don't stand off to the side and bark orders. They get in the mud with the troops. Great leaders are "people persons." They enjoy people. They relate well with people. They have winsome personalities. They inspire people to follow them through their own character and integrity. Great leaders know that if they have to establish their leadership position by declaring, "I am the leader," they have already lost their leadership position. Visionary leaders see the target, and they know the road that will take them there. They are adept at smoothing out the rough places in that road and straightening out the curves. When others fall away from the vision, the leader knows how to encourage them to take heart, overcome the obstacles, and rejoin the effort. He is careful not to run over people, but to respect people where they are, all the while showing them a better way.

> The conscientious, visionary pastor-leader sees his ministry in light of God's Kingdom and commits himself to be a Kingdom Christian.

For the pastor, visionary leadership is a must. He builds God's Kingdom through obedience to God's leadership in his own life. His understanding of God's will for the church comes through much prayer and devotion. He has a vision for the church and has shared that vision with the congregation.

The conscientious, visionary pastor-leader sees his ministry in light of God's Kingdom and commits himself to be a Kingdom Christian. He asks himself the same questions every Christian should ask:

- Kingdom Identity. Is a relationship with Christ my first priority? Is my personal conversion experience valid and vivid? Do I enjoy regular private devotion and public worship?

- Kingdom Commitment. Do I possess an unwavering, public commitment to Jesus as the only Lord and Savior of all?

- Kingdom Character. Is obedience to Christ's kingly rule evident in my conduct and lifestyle? In my language, in the stories I tell, in my relationships, and in my use of possessions?

- Kingdom Priority. Do I live for the sake of the King and His Kingdom? Are my energies directed to Christian aims? How do I spend my time and money? Am I willing to sacrifice for the cause of Christ?

- Kingdom Family. Are the principles of Christ lived out in my home? Do I honor my parents? Is my home life a positive testimony to the world? Do I honor my spouse and encourage her/him to walk with Christ? Am I modeling for my children a vibrant Christian life? Does my family have a spiritual purpose with definite Kingdom goals?

- Kingdom Perspective. Do I have an understanding of the comprehensive nature of the Kingdom of God? Am I willing to set aside lesser goals such as personal aggrandizement, economic prosperity, cultural or national stability, or other parochial or temporal aims? Do I carry out my ministry as part of the larger Kingdom enterprise? Do I value the ministry of other Christians as part of the Kingdom of God, even when I am not responsible for it and get no credit for it?

- Kingdom Calendar. Do I labor with a sense of urgency? Do I value the present opportunity, "redeeming the time, because the days are evil" (Ephesians 5:16 KJV)? [1]

The inclusion of the word "conscientious" in the title of this chapter is for the specific reason that it is not enough to be a visionary leader. A person may be a visionary leader and be lazy. He may have great ideas about what ought to be done, or what could be done, but unless he gets busy bringing that vision to reality, it means little. I fear that one of our greatest problems in ministry today is the lazy pastor. I have searched for some nice way to put that, but it escapes me. The pastor is in a position that, in many places, will allow him to sleep in with regularity. If he is not a self-starter, day after day can go by without much being accomplished.

A person may be a visionary leader and be lazy.

He is tempted to follow the lines of least resistance. He may realize that there are visits that need to be made, but he simply doesn't feel like it. He needs to start on next Sunday's messages, but he simply doesn't feel like it. He should go to the hospital to visit a church member, but he simply doesn't feel like it. "No one is going to say anything if I don't get that done right now. I'll just put it off until tomorrow." Oh, he's got some great ideas about what could happen, if he could only get this church of his to follow his leadership. They just don't seem to want to do anything. They are satisfied to come on Sundays and

---

1 "Empowering Kingdom Growth: Seeking First the King and His Kingdom," op. cit., p.3.

go through the motions of church, but there just seems to be a low level of commitment in the congregation. I wonder why?

I was recently inspired by a young pastor in our state. His name is Rick Brown. Rick is pastor at the Dunn Memorial Baptist Church in Baxley, Georgia, As soon as I arrived at his church on Sunday morning to preach for his congregation, he told me that he had just celebrated his 17th anniversary at the church. He said, "I want to show you what my church gave me for my anniversary." He led me around the corner of the church to the rear parking lot where he had parked his new Ford Ranger pickup truck. I bragged on how beautiful it was as we walked back to his church office. It was obvious that this church loved their pastor.

Dunn Memorial is a church that averages around 125 in weekly worship attendance, and this young man has served the church as pastor for 17 years. He is sharp, has a keen mind, and outstanding experience. I wondered if Rick might want to talk to me about leaving to go to another church. He had certainly been at his church for a respectable length of time; a move would not be out of the ordinary. He was undoubtedly capable of leading a larger church. I wondered why this relationship had lasted for 17 years while other pastors come and go through churches as though they had revolving doors. As I talked to him, however, I came to understand that he was in love with his church.

As we talked further in his office, I understood that it was not a lack of aspiration that kept him in his present position. He was energetic, fully engaged with his

> **He was energetic, fully engaged with his congregation and community, and excited about the future.**

congregation and community, and excited about the future.

I asked Rick to share with me a little about his schedule. He smiled as though he knew what I was thinking. Then he said, "Some people may think I'm a little crazy, but I get up at 4:30 every morning for my early morning run. By 6:00 o'clock I am in my office here at the church to spend time in study. I can get a lot accomplished at that hour of the morning because no one else is around, and the phone doesn't usually ring that early." He continued, "At 9:30 I stop by the local café where many of the lay folks gather for coffee and to talk and laugh. I always enjoy that time with folks from the community."

He went on to say that, in the late morning and early afternoon, he does his church visitation. At 4:15 every afternoon he has a live radio program for the community. He gets home about 5:00 every evening, but then, as every pastor knows, there are many evenings he is called back out for hospital emergencies, funerals, or other reasons.

I had the answer to my question about his longevity at the church. I thought to myself, "These folks have got to love and respect their pastor deeply. This self-starting pastor is like a gold mine to this church." I still wondered what had held his commitment to the church. I asked if he would tell me about the church. His eyes lit up with excitement as he told me that the church

> **"This self-starting pastor is like a gold mine to this church."**

is giving 36% of their unrestricted offerings to missions. Of that amount 27% goes to the Cooperative Program, 5% goes to the local association, and 4% goes to other missionaries. The church's vision is to increase the amount from 36% to 50% for missions. How wonderful!

Now I knew why Rick was happy in his church. He had been leading them energetically to grow as a great missions church. They had responded to that leadership, and he was as happy as he could be.

No doubt, Rick Brown is a visionary pastor, but that in itself is not enough. He is also conscientious and hardworking. There is no way around the hard work. If you are not willing to be a hard-working pastor, you are not going to have a healthy church. The people of your congregation who are people of integrity and hard work are going to resent lazy behavior. When the pastor is not working as hard to be an effective pastor as the lay people in the church have to work to be

> **"Frankly, there are so many things going on right now, I am having a difficult time keeping all the balls in the air."**

effective in their jobs, serious problems often erupt. The pastor has got to have it if he is to pastor a healthy church. What is it? It is conscientious, visionary leadership.

I was speaking to a frustrated pastor recently who confessed, "Frankly, there are so many things going on right now, I am having a difficult time keeping all the balls in the air." His comment certainly made sense to me, because much of the time, I find myself living with that kind of stress. It is important for the leader to be energetic, self-starting, and hard-working, but he must also strike a balance with other responsibilities such as his own personal family, health, friends, and spirit.

I commented to Janice the other day that I will forever be grateful to her for seeing that I always included in my schedule a balance of time for the family. She absolutely did the right thing in putting our daughters' various plays, music programs, and other performances at school on my church, and later, convention calendar. There were times when Kathy, Karen, and Jennifer were in elementary school that I would be one of the only dads present at the mid-morning program at Clark Elementary School. I'm sure I made a nuisance of myself with my video camera. I was the dad who walked up close to the stage to get those especially good shots. Many times when our girls would be performing during the halftime at football games on Friday nights, I would have to do a wedding rehearsal and then skip the dinner so I could take video of the girls. There were times that I got there just as the Drill Corps was marching out on the field, but I made it, and we cherish those tapes today. All our girls are grown and married with families of their own, but they still like to bring out the videotapes. They will sit for hours and look at those tapes and laugh and laugh at themselves.

We worked hard to preserve a family night each week. When our daughters were small, we would often rent a movie and have movie night. "Okay, girls," I would yell, "the movie is ready to start." They would come running, squealing with excitement. Then I would stop them at the entrance to the family room and ask for their tickets. "Tickets? We don't have any tickets, Daddy." "Well, you had better go make a ticket if you want to see the movie," I would say. Then they would go running off to their playroom to make tickets to get in the movie. They were very creative. The tickets were often drawn and colored and made to look like a movie ticket. I would wait for them, and before long, I would hear their little feet running down the stairs and toward the family room, laughing and squealing all the way. Janice would fix the popcorn and soft drinks. What fun we would have.

We also made sure that time was scheduled every year for family vacation. Most often we would go to the beach at Panama City or Destin, Florida. From the time that we got to the condominium until we left, the girls would be in the pool. I would do most of the cooking on vacation to give Janice a break, and I thoroughly enjoyed frying shrimp, crab claws, and fish. We enjoyed some amazing seafood dinners. Our rule was that the one who fixed dinner would not have to clean up, so the girls usually had the clean up duty. One year we took a trip in a borrowed RV. It was a 33-foot Pace Arrow. Janice and I enjoyed it greatly, but the girls complained quite a bit because, as teenagers, to them taking your vacation in an RV was not "cool." For several days we stayed in an old house at Montreat, North Carolina. The girls were not thrilled about that part of the trip either. The funny thing is, when they remember our vacations, they always go back to that vacation as one of the most memorable. We had some great times.

It is so important in the midst of your overwhelming leadership challenges that you not neglect your family and others you know and love.

85

It is so important in the midst of your overwhelming leadership challenges that you not neglect your family and others you know and love. I came across a piece on the Internet that speaks to this issue. It was written by Brian Dyson, CEO of Coca Cola Enterprises. It is a speech he delivered for a university commencement address several years ago. He titled it, "Life as a Juggler."

Imagine life as a game in which you are juggling some five balls in the air. You name them — work, family, health, friends and spirit—and you're keeping all of these in the air. You will soon understand that work is a rubber ball. If you drop it, it will bounce back. But the other four balls— family, health, friends and spirit—are made of glass. If you drop one of these, they will be irrevocably scuffed, marked, nicked, damaged or even shattered. They will never be the same. You must understand that and strive for balance in your life. How?

- Don't undermine your worth by comparing yourself with others. It is because we are different that each of us is special.

- Don't set your goals by what other people deem important. Only you know what is best for you.

- Don't take for granted the things closest to your heart. Cling to them as you would your life, for without them, life is meaningless.

- Don't let your life slip through your fingers by living in the past or for the future. By living your life one day at a time, you live ALL the days of your life.

- Don't give up when you still have something to give. Nothing is really over until the moment you stop trying.

- Don't be afraid to admit that you are less than perfect. It is this fragile thread that binds us to each other.

- Don't be afraid to encounter risks. It is by taking chances that we learn how to be brave.

- Don't shut love out of your life by saying it's impossible to find. The quickest way to receive love is to give; the fastest way to lose love is to hold it too tightly; and the best way to keep love is to give it wings.

- Don't run through life so fast that you forget not only where you've been, but also where you are going.

- Don't forget, a person's greatest emotional need is to feel appreciated.

- Don't be afraid to learn. Knowledge is weightless, a treasure you can always carry easily.

- Don't use time or words carelessly. Neither can be retrieved.

- Life is not a destination, but a journey to be savored every step of the way.[2]

Being called by God to serve as a spiritual leader in the life of the church is an overwhelming responsibility. Such a privilege demands no less than our very best effort. The leader should approach his responsibility with prayer, humility, joy, enthusiasm, commitment, and energy. There is no greater honor in this life than to be called by God to be one of His servant leaders. Pray that God will give you wisdom and a unique ability to discern His will so you might properly cast the vision for your church. Then with every ounce of commitment in you, accept the challenge to be a conscientious, visionary leader.

> **The leader should approach his responsibility with prayer, humility, joy, enthusiasm, commitment, and energy.**

2 Brian Dyson, "Life as a Juggler,"
   http://members.tripod.com/~ramgo/juggler.html

CHAPTER 5

QUALITY #5:
ENGAGE IN CHURCH
MULTIPLICATION

s I stood in the hallway at the door of my daughter's hospital room at University Hospital in Augusta, Georgia, I waited for what seemed like an eternity to hear some word about the birth of my second granddaughter. Then the news I awaited came in the form of a cry, a beautiful cry, the first sounds uttered by my new granddaughter. I said to John Bryan, my friend and my daughter and son-in-law's pastor, "She's here! She's really here!" My eyes filled with tears. God is so good, I thought as I praised the Lord and thanked Him for His graciousness to our family.

There is no miracle quite like the miracle of birth.

There is no miracle quite like the miracle of birth. Janice and I are blessed with two granddaughters, and, by the time this book is published, we expect to have a grandson.

We feel so blessed. Each one of our daughters was received as a gift from God. We have celebrated their lives since they took their first breath. We have rejoiced at every stage of their development. We celebrated God's goodness at each of their weddings. Now we have come to understand what "all the fuss is about" with regard to being grandparents. It really is special to hold those grandbabies in your arms, spoil them, and then give them back to their parents. Being a grandparent is a different experience.

Periodically, I remember what a friend told me a few years ago. I said, "Bill, I hear that your grandchildren have been visiting with you this week." He replied, "Yes, the little angels came in on Monday, and the little devils left on Saturday."

Every time a baby is born, God works a miracle. To me it is as much a miracle as the creation of the first man and first woman. "And the Lord God formed man of the dust of the ground, and breathed into his nostrils the breath of life; and man became a living soul" (Genesis 2:7 KJV). "And the Lord God caused a deep sleep to fall upon Adam, and he slept: and he took one of his ribs, and closed up the flesh instead thereof; And the rib, which the Lord God had taken from man, made he a woman, and brought her unto the man. And Adam said, This is now bone of my bones, and flesh of my flesh: she shall be called Woman, because she was taken out of Man" (Genesis 2:21-23 KJV).

When God created Adam and Eve, He gave them a very special assignment which is reported in Genesis 1:28 KJV: "And God blessed them, and God said unto them, Be fruitful and multiply, and replenish the earth, and subdue it: and have dominion over the fish of the sea, and over the

All healthy organisms are blessed with the capacity to multiply.

fowl of the air, and over every living thing that moveth upon the earth."

The command to procreate is in keeping with God's creation. All healthy organisms are blessed with the capacity to multiply. While the verbiage is quite different, the command to the Church is very similar. Jesus said, "All power is given unto me in heaven and in earth. Go ye therefore, and teach all nations, baptizing them in the name of the Father, and of the Son, and of the Holy Ghost: Teaching them to observe all things whatsoever I have commanded you: and, lo, I am with you always, even unto the end of the world" (Matthew 28:18-20 KJV).

> **"When we plant new churches, we ought to genetically encode them to reproduce themselves."**

When I came to my present position with the Georgia Baptist Convention, I went through an orientation at what was then the Home Mission Board, but is now the North American Mission Board of the Southern Baptist Convention. In that orientation Charles Chaney said something that deeply impacted me. I had never heard anything like this statement before. Chaney said, "When we plant new churches, we ought to genetically encode them to reproduce themselves." He went on to talk about the powerful impact of multiplication. So many churches that have been planted were not planted with a sense of calling to reproduce themselves.

Chaney has identified the following problems that seemed to plague Southern Baptist church planting efforts during the 20 years that he has served in denominational leadership:

- Few top quality leaders
- Inadequate and often inappropriate training
- Inadequate human support systems
- Too many wounded soldiers
- Too few churches committed to reproduction
- An unacceptable success rate
- Practicing addition, not multiplication
- Wrong attitudes toward buildings
- Restrictive paradigms that keep churches from multiplying.[1]

If you asked congregations why they have never reproduced, they would likely give you a list of "reasons" which would really be more like a list of phobias about church planting. The following list suggests some of these phobias, and what can be done to overcome them:

WE ARE TOO SMALL.

Rationale: Small churches are not equipped to start new congregations. They do not have enough resources to support a new church.

Solution: Believe that a church of any size is capable of starting anything the Lord leads them to start. Whatever the Lord commands us to do, He will lead us to do by providing all that we need to accomplish His will. If the Lord gives you a vision to start a new congregation, begin with prayer and a recommitment to His Lordship.

1 "Barriers To Church Planting," Multiplying Church Networks Orientation and Training Manual, Church Planting Group: North American Mission Board of the Southern Baptist Convention, Alpharetta, Georgia, p. 2.

THERE ARE ALREADY ENOUGH CHURCHES.

Rationale: There are churches of every kind everywhere. You cannot drive a mile without passing by a church.

Solution: Discover for yourself the number of people that attend churches in a given community. Gather this information by simply asking each church. From this information, determine the number of lost people in the community. Remember that new churches reach more people than existing ones. This could become an exciting venture.

IT WILL DRAIN OUR FINANCES.

Rationale: Starting a church can be expensive. You have to provide salary for a new pastor, raise money to rent a meeting place or buy one, and purchase equipment and supplies.

Solution: How much value do you put on the salvation of lost people? Most Christians believe that one lost person saved is worth the money spent. As a result, when given a clear vision for a new church start, church members will go the extra mile to support the new church.

IT WILL SPLIT MY CHURCH.

Rationale: If we start a new church, we will lose good workers from our church. If we lose them, we will also lose valuable resources.

Solution: Remember the dynamics of giving. The more you give, the more you will receive in return.

View the workers that leave as a love offering to the Lord. Also, this will give opportunities for other church members to step forward into leadership roles. Of course, the Lord will send new workers to the church.

WE NEED TO STRENGTHEN OUR CHURCH FIRST.

Rationale: We need all the people we can get to help us develop and strengthen this church. After we are strong enough, we can help start a new congregation.

Solution: At the very core of the church is the heart for lost people to come to know Christ as Savior. If an unchurched community or people group has been identified, the Spirit of the Lord will move His church to respond. The best possible option is the birthing of a new church. Starting a new congregation will help members become more concerned about their lost neighbors, which will cause the church to grow stronger.

MY MEMBERS WILL NOT SUPPORT IT.

Rationale: My people do not have a desire to start a new church. They feel comfortable with where the church is. It meets their needs.

Solution: Begin slowly with the key leaders. Create awareness by sharing population growth, churched and unchurched ratios, and the benefits of starting new congregations. After support is gained from a few of the key leaders, develop a process you will follow to bring everyone on board. At each step of the process, make sure you broaden the participation. This will create ownership of the new work. It will also begin developing a church planting DNA that will consume the church for future church plants.

WE DO NOT HAVE A VISION FOR IT.
Rationale: We just do not see a need to start a new church. If other churches want to do this, I am sure the Lord will bless them for it. We enjoy our church family and the fellowship that exists here. We definitely want to see people get saved, but not by starting a new church.

Solution: Most churches have some sort of outreach ministries. Utilize this heart for missions by expanding on it. Expose church members to ministries that lead to new church starts. For example, get the church to conduct a Vacation Bible School or block party in a developing neighborhood; adopt a church planter; join a church that is in the process of starting a new congregation. From these mission activities, look for opportunities to create a desire for your members to do likewise.

We just do not see a need to start a new church.

WE CANNOT FIND CHURCH PLANTERS.
Rationale: It is crucial to have the right leadership to begin a new church. This has made it difficult for

us to consider starting a church. We want to make sure we have a good church planting experience.

Solution: Discover a church planting organization that has a good farm system for church planters. Make sure the organization has a good assessment and training system for potential church planters. Also, remember that some of the best church planters come from within the harvest. This means that God might be raising up a leader from the community where the new church will be planted.

WE DO NOT KNOW HOW TO START A CHURCH.

Rationale: When you start a project, you generally have a plan in place. You know the steps, obstacles and even some shortcuts. If you do not know what you are doing, the project will usually take more time and money, and in the end, it will not look as good as it could have. We really do not know how to start a church.

Solution: The greatest teacher of church planting is experience. Begin by networking with experienced church planters. They are the most valuable tools for knowing how to start a church. You might inquire about existing networks of church planters or sponsoring churches. Learn from these people for at least a year before you start putting your plans together. During this time of preparation, consider attending two or three training events for church planters. You will not only learn, but you will be inspired. As you go, do not forget to take some of your key leaders.

WE ARE AFRAID OF FAILING.

Rationale: Anytime a church fails at anything they do, there is a great repercussion. It creates disharmony and disappointments that are difficult to overcome. The reason is that you are dealing with volunteers and not paid staff. In this failure, you generally lose good people who either move to another church or become less active. Starting a church is a scary thing. You do not know whether it is going to grow or die.

Solution: There is a need to occasionally revisit these things: Why are you a Christian? What were you called to do? What is the purpose or mission of the church? We have been called to be on mission for our Lord. The Spirit within us compels us to continually move forward to share the Gospel with unreached communities. Time is short and we must take the Gospel to people today. Today may be the only time they have left. Church planting is one of the greatest outreach tools available to the church today.[2]

> **Church planting is one of the greatest outreach tools available to the church today**

One of the greatest joys I have had as executive director of a state Baptist convention is working with the Administration Committee of our Executive Committee to grant funds on a monthly basis to new church starts. There are close to 100 new Anglo, African-American, and

---

2 Ibid, pp. 2-6.

97

ethnic church plants each year. What a joy it is to grant money to assist with the purchase of property, the pastor's salary, and mobile chapels to be used temporarily until the church is strong enough to build. The Convention also helps new churches with their first loan. It is often difficult for a new church to get a loan through conventional channels, so the Convention steps up to the plate with significant loan assistance. These loans bear no interest for the first six months and, thereafter, are at highly competitive interest rates.

If you wish to start a new church, but don't know how it could possibly happen, understand that there is always a way if it is God's will. I remember a few years ago when I was approached by Jerry Baker of our Language Missions Department and Sid Hopkins, associational missionary for the Gwinnett Metro Baptist Association in the Atlanta metropolitan area, about a challenge we were facing with new ethnic starts. Apparently, there were not enough churches able to provide meeting space for the new ethnic congregations. Jerry and Sid shared with me the idea they had about establishing an International Ministry Center for the purpose of nurturing new ethnic congregations. In short, the Convention partnered with the association on the innovative project. The Convention purchased nine acres of property for the center. The Association committed funds for the modular buildings that would house the new congregations. The congregations would use the facilities until they became strong enough to purchase their own property and build their first unit. Since the structures at the International Ministry Center are modular, if the congregation wished to do so, they could purchase the church building and move it with them to their new site. This creative idea has made it possible for numerous ethnic congregations to get a start that may have otherwise been unable to do so.

The truth of the matter is, every congregation can participate in church multiplication. Even if church multiplication has never been a part of your church's mission and ministry, it is possible for you to add this new and exciting dimension to your ministry. You can be a parenting church or a partnering church. Parenting churches are involved in direct church planting. Partnering churches partner with others to start new churches. This can be done several ways. One form of partnering that is gaining strength today is partnering with a cluster of churches to plant a new congregation. These cluster groups can encourage each other. The group with representatives from several different churches meets regularly to pray about planting a new church. They share their common vision and sense of God's leadership to have an impact on an area or people group. They work together to develop a strategy for the new start. They share people and financial resources to make the vision a reality.

The truth of the matter is, every congregation can participate in church multiplication.

Another approach is to partner with the association to plant a new church. Similar to the cluster group, the association brings the strength of a number of churches to bear upon the new start vision. There is strength in numbers and the effort to start a new church is surely strengthened by increased participation.

It should also be mentioned that the denomination has been a partner in many church starts around the country. If you wish to start a church outside of your geographic area, great care is encouraged to make others aware of what you intend to do. State conventions and associations will be helpful in working with your church, cluster of churches, or association to make your vision a reality. Further, those who are closer to the geographic area in which you have interest will be able to caution you about possible pitfalls that could sabotage your efforts.

Recently, I was invited by leadership at the North American Mission Board and Lifeway Christian Resources to chair a taskforce that is planning the Southern Baptist Convention's emphasis for the year 2005. We have had numerous meetings of this group of Southern Baptists from across the country. Our discussions have been enthusiastic as we anticipate a great year of harvest in 2005. While we are not setting numeric goals for churches, associations or conventions, we do have goals that we are praying will be attained: 1,000,000 baptized; 100,000 new Sunday School units started; and 2,500 new churches planted. We trust God to provide 1,000,000 people, signed up over the Internet, to pray daily for the Southern Baptist Convention beginning in 2003. During 2004, we will ask that every Southern Baptist church provide witness training for their members during that year. And then in 2005, we pray that we will see 1,000,000 new believers baptized. Rather than be the culminating

1,000,000 baptized; 100,000 new Sunday School units started; and 2,500 new churches planted.

year of a program, we would like to see 2005 as the beginning year of a movement of God among His people.

Recently, a survey of 1,000 pastors was conducted by the North American Mission Board regarding the strategy and goals for the 2005 emphasis. At the time of this writing, responses have been received from 300 pastors. Researcher Phil Jones states that this is a typical response for this group of respondents and type of survey. Major findings include:

- Ninety-five percent of pastors agree, "…it is time for a stronger cooperative emphasis focusing on evangelism, church planting and discipleship." Nearly two-thirds strongly agree with this statement.

> **Ninety-five percent of pastors agree, "…it is time for a stronger cooperative emphasis focusing on evangelism, church planting and discipleship."**

- Four out of five pastors indicate that their congregations have an intentional plan for reaching the lost and unchurched in their community.

- Nine out of ten pastors indicate it is important for Southern Baptists to develop national and local advertising aimed at sharing the Good News of Jesus Christ with the general public – three out of four think it is very important.

- Nine out of ten pastors indicate it is important for Southern Baptists to promote the planting of new congregations.

- Twenty-four percent of pastors responding to the survey indicated that their church was involved in planting or sponsoring a new church.

- Two-thirds of pastors responding indicated their churches started one or more Bible study units during 2001. Only about a third of these new units were started in a location other than in their church building (or the place they normally meet for worship).

- Three out of four pastors report that their congregation would consider working with other churches to be part of a cooperative emphasis focusing on evangelism, church planting and discipleship. One out of three is completely behind this approach.

- Almost two-thirds of pastors indicate that promoting convention goals such as 1,000,000 baptisms, 1,000,000 persons praying, 100,000 new Bible study units, 2,500 church plants, etc., is helpful when their church is participating in a cooperative emphasis. Three out of ten indicate goals do not matter, goals have no relevance or they are neutral regarding this issue. Only a small 4% of pastors indicate that Convention goals are unhelpful or hinder meaningful participation.[3]

---

3 Phil Jones, "Survey of 1,000 Pastors for the 2005 Emphasis," North American Mission Board of the Southern Baptist Convention, Alpharetta, Georgia, June 3, 2002, pp. 1-2.

While there may be varying levels of interest in planting a new church, it is a distinctive of the New Testament that we are to take seriously. Jesus commissioned us to go into all the world with the Gospel and make disciples, baptizing them and teaching them. Clearly, this is a function of the church, which was established by Christ to proclaim the Good News that Jesus Christ is the Son of the living God. Our focus should be laser-like upon the spreading of the Gospel. Further, the Apostle Paul faithfully went about planting New Testament churches and literally turning the world of his day toward Jesus Christ.

Paul established churches as he was led by the Holy Spirit. In fact, we observe one of the clearest representations of how we are led by the Spirit of God from Paul's experience reported in Acts 16:6-8 KJV: "Now when they had gone throughout Phrygia and the region of Galatia, and were forbidden of the

Paul established churches as he was led by the Holy Spirit.

Holy Ghost to preach the word in Asia, After they were come to Mysia, they assayed to go into Bithynia: but the Spirit suffered them not. And they passing by Mysia came down to Troas."

It was immediately thereafter that Paul experienced the vision of the man from Macedonia calling for Paul to "Come over into Macedonia and help us" (Acts 16:9 KJV). From that point forward Paul would enter upon a missionary journey that would lead him to Philippi where he would plant a new church. It would become his most beloved congregation.

From there Paul traveled through Amphipolis and Apollonia and went directly to Thessalonica, a major commercial city of his day, where Paul knew that if he could establish a new church, the impact of the Gospel could spread throughout the entire Roman Empire. Indeed, he did plant a wonderful church at Thessalonica in the midst of persecution. In spite of the persecution, the church would thrive.

From Thessalonica, Paul traveled to Berea, where he preached in the synagogue, and there resulted a truly remarkable revival among the people with many coming to Christ.

From there Paul went to Athens, where he preached among the philosophers on Mars' hill. You will recall the reaction of the philosophers when they heard Paul speak of the resurrection of Christ. Some rejected the Gospel; others said that they would like to hear more about it, but at a later time. Still, others believed.

From Athens Paul went to Corinth, where he preached in the synagogue for a long while. The Bible says, "...many of the Corinthians hearing believed, and were baptized" (Acts 18:8b KJV).

So it was that Paul faithfully preached the Gospel and planted churches throughout Asia Minor and would customarily return to those congregations to encourage them in the faith. In Paul we have an outstanding model for church multiplication. People are no less hungry for the Gospel of Christ today. While we believe our world to be more complicated today than what Paul faced, the persecution which daily endangered his life is not a hindrance that we experience in the United States today.

People need the Lord. The truth is that wherever the Gospel is preached, people are saved. The events of our world have created more openness to the Gospel than we have likely witnessed in our lifetime, or the lifetime of our parents or grandparents. The time is right to advance with the Gospel.

The events of our world have created more openness to the Gospel than we have likely witnessed in our lifetime, or the lifetime of our parents or grandparents.

Planting churches, then, is relevant because of a number of factors:

- More than 170,000,000 people in America are lost. Planting churches will accelerate the rate of winning people to Jesus.

- Planting churches is the most effective way to reach unchurched people. One estimate indicated that 60% of adults who joined new congregations were not active in church immediately before joining.

- New congregations grow faster than established congregations. They reach about two-and-one-half times more people per member than older churches.

- Additional church units are necessary to reach the growing population. At the current yearly rate of one baptism for every 27 resident members, Southern Baptist Churches would need 441 years to reach today's lost population.

- People sometimes perceive traditions of older churches to be barriers to participation. Some people may be more likely to attend and participate in a new church that does not have traditions.

- Mission churches are needed in places where spiritual vacuums result from churches moving out of the area.

- Racial and ethnic groups need churches that recognize their background, language and cultural needs.

- Pockets of people may be missed by churches. Some people groups, because of lifestyle, socioeconomic status, or other reasons, may not respond to existing churches. A new church can use approaches related to the immediate needs of these groups.

- Communities with large numbers of unchurched people need evangelical congregations.

- Housing patterns may be a hindrance to reaching people. A new congregation may be needed within a housing development, multi-housing unit or high-rise.

- New communities and newly developed areas need new congregations.

- New congregations enlist additional people to work in Kingdom business, providing opportunities for expanded Christian service and growth.

- Multiplying congregations means multiplying Christian workers, missionaries, baptisms, witnessing church members, Bible study groups, mission support and spiritual growth.

- Planting congregations opens new doors for people to enter the church.[4]

Jesus commanded us to reach our world with the Gospel. New churches reach people for Christ at a more rapid rate than older churches. Our nation is 60% unchurched and getting more lost with the passing of every day. We need more ethnic churches to reach the swelling tide of ethnicity in our country. Planting a new church stimulates the involvement of members in the parent church. For these reasons and many more, it seems that church multiplication is a no-brainer. The evidence seems conclusive, doesn't it?

New churches reach people for Christ at a more rapid rate than older churches.

---

4 "Plan Book for Churches Starting Churches: Seven Steps to Planting A Church," Appendix A: Church Planting Rationale: The Need for New Congregations, North American Mission Board of the Southern Baptist Convention, Alpharetta, Georgia, 2000, p.26.

CHAPTER 6

QUALITY #6:
AN ENVIRONMENT OF
UNITY AND JOY

*A*fter the ascension of Christ, the disciples gathered in the upper room in Jerusalem where Acts 1:14 KJV says, "These all continued with one accord in prayer and supplication, with the women, and Mary the mother of Jesus, and with his brethren." Then a few verses further into Acts, it says that "...they were all with one accord in one place" (Acts 2:1 KJV). Then in Acts 2:46 KJV, it states, "And they, continuing daily with one accord in the temple, and breaking bread from house to house, did eat their meat with gladness and singleness of heart." What a great church this was! In the midst of persecution, they continuously expressed their love for the Lord and their love for each other. "Gladness and singleness of heart" are great words to be spoken of any congregation. These words indicate a healthy congregation. By the way, you can tell when you walk through the door of a church if that church is characterized by "gladness and singleness of heart."

> **By the way, you can tell when you walk through the door of a church if that church is characterized by "gladness and singleness of heart."**

I am frequently asked by people who do not understand what the executive director of a state convention does: "Which church do you pastor?" They always have a surprised expression on their faces when I tell them that I don't pastor a church. I relate to all of our Georgia Baptist churches. Then they are puzzled further when I tell them that I preach in a different church every Sunday. Sometimes I get the distinct impression that they are saying silently, "Okay, so you are not really in the ministry, right?" No, I really am in the ministry, and I really do preach in a different church every week. That exposure to different churches has been educational and many times very inspiring. There are unhealthy situations, though, that I encounter from time to time, and usually I am unaware until I arrive at the church. When I walk in the door, I can tell a lot about the church. I am not saying that because I am unusually perceptive. This is not about acute perception. What I am saying is, if I can sense that something is not right, other people who visit the church can also tell when they walk into the church for the first time.

Sometimes as I arrive, I am greeted warmly before I ever get to the entrance of the building. This is a good sign. Often when I walk in the door, there are friendly people going about their Sunday morning responsibilities with a smile on their faces. They often recognize that I am not a "regular" and cordially greet me. Others recognize me and extend a warm greeting. Recently, I arrived at a church to preach at their worship service and a nice senior adult gentleman had obviously been posted at the door to watch for my arrival. When I reached for the door, he threw it open and said, "Dr. White, I am so glad to see you! Welcome to our church. I am going to show you to our pastor's study where he is looking forward to visiting with you before the worship service. Can I get you some water, coffee or a coke? The restrooms are just down the hall on the right. Once again, thank you for coming to our church. We are looking forward to your message." I've got to tell you, it made me feel like a million dollars. It made me feel cared for, loved, appreciated. I don't care who you are, you should feel those emotions when you walk through the door of any church.

The contrast is that, on occasion, I have entered undetected and wandered the halls until I found someone to ask, "Do you know where I might find the pastor?" Response: "No, not really." "Well, can you tell me where his office is located?" "No. I don't know where it is." "Okay, no problem, I'll find him. It's nice to see you. Are you doing well this morning?" (No reply). This is not a good indication. Now, of course, sometimes you may initially run into someone who just is not having a good morning.

Think of your visitors.
Think of your visitors.
Think of your visitors.

Think of your visitors. Think of your visitors. Think of your visitors. What will be their immediate impressions when they arrive at your church? Will they be greeted before they even reach the entrance? Will there be someone at the entrance to extend a warm hand of greeting? Will they offer assistance to the person in helping them get to their Sunday School class or to the sanctuary or worship center? If one is not familiar with the church and may not know anyone who attends the church, showing up at the front door of the church on Sunday is a huge step. Why not have friendly people on hand to make the visitor's introduction to the church a memorable experience?

When I began seminary at The Southern Baptist Theological Seminary in Louisville, Kentucky, Janice and I had been married for only a couple of weeks. The first Sunday we were there, we went to a church for the morning worship service. Of course, we were also looking for a church where we might place our membership. This first Sunday was not a good experience. We parked our car, walked up the front steps of the church and in the front door, found our way into the sanctuary, and sat down. The sanctuary was pretty full that morning. We were a little surprised when the minister of music came out onto the platform before the worship service and began to rehearse the congregation in the singing of a new hymn so that we would "get it right" during the actual worship service. Neither of us had ever experienced anything like that.

During the worship service there was a time for greeting the visitors, but nobody greeted us. We were packed in with members of the church seated all around us. We did raise our hands at the appropriate time to indicate that we were visitors. We both placed the visitor's ribbon on our clothing as requested so that we might be identified as guests. At the conclusion of the service, we walked slowly out as the crowd filled the aisle. I am sad to say that, from the time we walked up the front steps of the church until the time we walked out to our car, not a single person ever spoke to us. No one. Not the people seated around us. Not an usher. Not a staff member. No one. As I recall, we did receive a form letter from the pastor the following week telling us how glad he was that we had visited and hoped that we would return and possibly consider joining their church.

> **From the time we walked up the front steps of the church until the time we walked out to our car, not a single person ever spoke to us.**

As newlyweds, we needed a warm and friendly place to worship. We were embarking on our life together and on a several year journey at the seminary. We were looking for a good church that would provide the strength and assurance we would need along the way. The form letter was several days too late. When we left the church that morning, we looked at each other and said, "Well, we can check that one off our list." Now that is a fairly blunt response, but families usually do tell it like it is without mincing words. Don't ever let anyone leave your church saying, "We can check that one off our list," because not a single person spoke to them from the time they arrived until the time they left. Be the friendly, receiving church that visitors are looking for when they visit your church.

I might mention that when I went to First Baptist Paducah, Kentucky, I continued a practice that my predecessor began. On Sunday afternoon, I would telephone all the visitors who had worshiped with us in the morning worship services. Usually there was a pretty good-sized stack of visitor's cards, but it never took a long time to complete the task. The comments I received from that Sunday afternoon ministry were phenomenal. Most people were amazed that I would take the time to give them a call to express how much we enjoyed having them in worship that morning at First Baptist. They felt appreciated and certainly knew from the effort that they were welcome and wanted in our church.

Think for a moment about the people you most like to be with. Are they happy people, or sad? Are they people with a positive attitude, or a negative attitude? Unless something is unusual about you, I am confident that you will say that you choose to be around people who are happy people and who have a positive attitude. Why, then, would you want to join a church that is a sad church with a negative attitude? Generally speaking, people will not choose to join a church like this. They are going to choose to worship where they can be around happy people with a positive attitude about life and serving the Lord through His church. Be the church that you would choose if you were new in your community seeking a church home.

Be the church that you would choose if you were new in your community seeking a church home.

Another matter related to being a happy and positive church has to do with the way church members treat one another. An old adage says that if you have two Baptists together, you will have three opinions on any one subject. While repeating that adage consistently gets a laugh, I don't like having that reputation. Why should we be satisfied to come across as contentious people?

Jesus said, "A new commandment I give to you, that you love one another, even as I have loved you, that you also love one another. By this all men will know that you are My disciples, if you have love for one another" (John 13:34-35 NASB). "Two Baptists, three opinions?" Yes, sometimes it is that way, but we should be able to disagree without being disagreeable. Paul put it this way: "I, therefore, the prisoner of the Lord, entreat you to walk in a manner worthy of the calling with which you have been called, with all humility and gentleness, with patience, showing forbearance to one another in love, being diligent to preserve the unity of the Spirit in the bond of peace" (Ephesians 4:1-3 NASB).

Notice that the emphasis is upon unity, not uniformity. Unity speaks of being together. Uniformity speaks of being alike. We are not all alike. There are varying opinions on many subjects. It seems that the key to lasting fellowship is to recognize that there are people who disagree with you and that is okay. God didn't use a cookie cutter when He made us. The wonderful thing about being a Baptist is when a matter is before the church, it is discussed, and then a vote is taken to determine the outcome of the matter. Of course, it should be understood that one matter that is not up for debate is the truth of God's Word. This requires no vote. Those who wish to vote in contradiction to the Bible are "out of order"!

From the time I was a child, I have been tuned in to Baptist polity. I remember my father advising me, "There may be varying opinions on a matter before the church, and that's fine, but when the church discusses the issue and then votes, that decides the matter. At that point, everyone should leave the church united behind the decision of the church, even if your side didn't win the vote." That is good counsel, and that is, in fact, the way it should work. Unfortunately, many times it does not work that way. People disagree. A vote is taken. Then the people whose opinion did not win the day leave the business meeting disgruntled, mad at the church, mad at the world. For

This is not your kingdom that is being built; it is the Kingdom of God.

weeks they hang around in the corners of the hallways of the church spreading their sour attitude among the members, creating discord in the church. This kind of strategy has no good conclusion.

Let's all be reminded that it's not about you; it's about God. This is not your kingdom that is being built; it is the Kingdom of God. We can get so wrapped up in our opinion of the way things should be that we completely forget that the church is about God's business. We are building His Kingdom.

The Apostle Paul dealt with a touchy situation in the church where there was a conflict among the members over their heroes. The problem was that they forgot Who all of this was about in the first place. "For when one says, 'I am of Paul,' and another, 'I am of Apollos,' are you not mere men? What then is Apollos? And what is Paul? Servants through whom you believed, even as the Lord gave opportunity to each one. I planted, Apollos watered, but God was causing the growth. So then neither the one who plants nor the one who waters is anything, but God who causes the growth" (1 Corinthians 3:4-7 NASB).

116

Then the ninth verse says, "For we are laborers together with God" (1 Corinthians 3:9a KJV).

This is God's wonderful work in which we are involved. What a privilege it is to be allowed to be co-laborers with God for His Kingdom. It is too easy to forget this in the day-to-day affairs of the church. Then it becomes "my church," "my plans," "my committee," "my budget," "my buildings," "my staff." An environment of unity and joy results when the members of the church are all working together in unity for the same cause, the advancement of the Kingdom of God.

It is also beneficial to remember that we have the same background. While the members of the church are all unique, there is at least one thing that we all have in common—we are sinners saved by grace. This commonality should cause us to understand that there is no place in the church for an attitude of superiority or exclusivity. In one of the revisions of our Baptist Hymnal, the words for the hymn "At the Cross" were changed. The old wording "for such a worm as I" was changed to "sinners such as I." Perhaps we should have left the worm in the hymn. The worm is certainly in all of us and, except for the wonderful grace of Jesus, we would be hopelessly lost. "There is none righteous, no, not one" (Romans 3:10 KJV). Therefore, we shouldn't act self-righteous because everyone knows we're not. There is no place in the church for a holier-than-thou attitude. Our common nature should create an uncommon unity among us. We are brothers and sisters, and we should also be friends.

Several years ago during summer vacation, Dr. Charles Fuller and his family were staying in a Georgia

117

motel. After dinner, Dr. Fuller's two sons, ages thirteen and ten, were swimming in the motel pool. The older son met another boy who was also traveling with his family. After playing in the pool with the older Fuller boy, the new friend noticed that there was some kind of special relationship between him and the younger boy also in the pool. So he asked, "Who is your friend?" The older son looked around and then answered, "Who, him? He's not my friend; he's my brother."

When as brothers and sisters in Jesus Christ, we focus our efforts on working together for the common cause of proclaiming Christ to a lost world and discipling believers, then we experience unity. It is through our common experience of the saving grace of the Lord that we have joy. This unity and joy should permeate the fellowship of the church in such a way that whenever anyone attends our church, they know immediately that this is a healthy family of faith that finds its joy in serving the Lord with "gladness and singleness of heart." They should feel it from the time they get out of their cars and walk through the door of the church.

CHAPTER 7

QUALITY #7: CHEERFUL STEWARDSHIP

I enjoyed growing up in a pastor's home. There were many events that took place at the church that I was able to attend as part of the pastor's family. I was never big on sitting through the weddings, but I did enjoy the receptions. The wedding cake was my favorite. I always loved that white icing. Wedding cake icing has a very special taste. In fact, I was pretty much a cake, punch, and nuts kind of guy. I had enough of it growing up to make me a connoisseur of reception cuisine. This was one reason I was so shocked when my daughters grew up and planned their weddings. I was under the impression that cake, punch, and nuts were still the top of the line. If you wanted to get extravagant, you might add a silver tray of those little round mints with the tiny iced flowers on top of them.

What a shock it was to learn how far behind I was. Now, I was told, you are supposed to feed people at the reception. "Dad, you can't have cake, punch, and nuts at a wedding reception any more. You have things like boiled shrimp, meat balls in marinara sauce, cheese balls with five or six different kinds of crackers, hot wings, prime rib, baked ham, vegetables with several different kinds of dip."

119

They would rattle off this information like they owned a catering service. "But what about the cake, punch, and nuts?" I would ask. "Oh, sure, Dad, we'll have plenty of cake, punch, and nuts just for you." I can tell you that I had no idea what I was getting myself into when baby girls started arriving at our house. So, three times for three daughters, we put on a pretty big spread and ate leftovers out of little white cardboard boxes for weeks.

On more than one occasion, I was standing near enough to my dad at a wedding reception to hear a conversation between the groom and my father. Dad's remarks were always the same. The nervous groom would stammer out the words, "Dr. White, what do I owe you?" Dad would reply, "Whatever you think she's worth."

> **"Whatever you think she's worth."**

It was especially enjoyable to watch the unfolding event if the bride was near enough to hear this conversation. She would look at the groom to see what he would do next, and how much he thought she was worth. It was a pretty good response to an otherwise ill-timed question.

You know, of course, that the church is the Bride of Christ. There have been plenty of people who ask a similar question as they contemplate what they should give to the church. "How much should I give to my church?" "Whatever you think she's worth!" How valuable is the Bride of Christ to you? I'm sure God wearies of questions about whether one should tithe on the gross or the net of his income. Give what you think she's worth. "God, you know I've had a lot of expenses with our new car and new boat all having to be paid for at the same time." Give whatever you think she's worth. "God, you know we are really strapped for dollars because of our over-sized house payment." Give whatever you think she's worth. Paul puts it plainly: "Let each one do just as he has purposed in his heart; not grudgingly or under compulsion; for God loves a cheerful giver" (2 Corinthians 9:7 NASB).

My wife and I are members at North Metro First Baptist Church in Lawrenceville, Georgia, where Dr. Frank Cox is senior pastor. Frank and his wife, Mary, are two of God's special people. I enjoy being able to be in my church for worship, but because I am usually preaching somewhere, I rarely get to attend my own church. After being away for many weeks, I had the happy occasion of being able to be a worshiper at my church one Sunday morning. I was not prepared for a change that Frank had initiated in our worship service. When it came time for the morning offering, Frank stepped to the side of the pulpit and announced, "It's time to receive the morning offering." The congregation erupted in applause. I was shocked. I had never heard a congregation applaud over the opportunity to give to the Lord. At first, I didn't know what to think.

> **I had never heard a congregation applaud over the opportunity to give to the Lord.**

Then I said to myself, "You know, the Bible says that God loves a cheerful giver." Literally, the verse says that God loves a hilarious giver, so I think this is just about right. You may say, "Well, that wouldn't happen in our church. We don't clap." That's okay. What about saying "Amen" when the pastor announces that it is time to receive the offering? "No, that wouldn't work either. We don't say 'Amen' in our church either." Well, what about smiling and nodding your head when the pastor announces that it is time to receive the offering? At the very least, there should be a feeling of great joy in our hearts when it comes time to give our offering to the Lord.

As a high school young person, I enjoyed hanging around with my father while he shook hands following the morning worship service at First Baptist Church in Montgomery, Alabama. After the last person left the church, he and I would walk back to the church office and then on to his car where we would ride together on our way home to Sunday dinner. I remember one particular Sunday around the first of the year. After Dad had shaken the last person's hand, he and I walked back through the now-darkened sanctuary. Col. Pete Summer, one of our fine laymen, a deacon and a colonel at Maxwell Air Force Base, was standing in the center aisle waiting for Dad so he could talk to him privately. Sensing his desire for a personal conversation, I stopped short while he and Dad began to converse. Though I was several feet away, I could still hear what was being said, and I have always been so glad that I did. Pete said, "Pastor, when we had our stewardship commitment time last year, I was pleased to sign a commitment card. This year has been an unusually difficult year for our family though, and I was not able to live up to my commitment. I am sharing this with you, not to brag in any way, but to let you know what a wonderful worship experience I had this morning. Since I had fallen behind in my tithe commitment, I went to the bank this past week and borrowed the money to make up the difference in my tithe. I gave that tithe to the Lord this morning and my heart is filled to overflowing with joy. I just had to share it with you." Then Pete said

> **"I don't mind owing the bank, but I don't want to owe my Lord."**

this, "I don't mind owing the bank, but I don't want to owe my Lord." What a tremendous statement that was! "I don't mind owing the bank, but I don't want to owe my Lord."

That one statement has influenced my heart more regarding stewardship than any sermon series I have heard or preached on Christian stewardship. God truly loves a cheerful giver. Cheerful stewardship is clearly a characteristic of healthy churches.

God has a plan for the support of His Kingdom work. It is the tithe. If God's people will follow God's plan, there will always be an abundance of resources to do God's work. Long ago, the prophet Malachi declared what we are to give to God, where we are to give it, and what we might expect to happen when we are faithful. "Bring ye all the tithes into the storehouse, that there may be meat in mine house, and prove me now herewith, saith the Lord of hosts, if I will not open you the windows of heaven, and pour you out a blessing, that there shall not be room enough to receive it" (Malachi 3:10 KJV).

I remember the day one of the young men in a church I was serving as pastor came to my office to argue with me about the tithe. I had just preached on the Scriptural mandate to tithe one-tenth of our income to God. This young man was a high achiever. He was what we called in that day a "Yuppie." He was living in the right kind of house and driving the right kind of car to be recognized as an up-and-coming young executive. He said, "The tithe is the law of the Old Testament. The New Testament did away with the tithe." Now, before I go further, let me say in fairness that this young man is not the only one who has ever argued that with me. I will also say that no one has ever argued that point with me because he wanted to give more than the tithe. If the New Testament teaches anything, it teaches that we are to give the tithe and then go beyond the tithe to give offerings to the Lord. In Matthew 23:23 NASB, Jesus commended the tithe: "Woe to you, scribes and Pharisees, hypocrites! For you tithe mint and dill and cummin, and have neglected the weightier provisions of the law: justice and mercy and faithfulness; but these are the things you should have done without neglecting the others."

Jesus was not saying, "Don't tithe." He was saying, "Do tithe." But in the process of fulfilling the law, don't overlook the greater matters such as being just, merciful and faithful in your dealings with others and with God. It's interesting that Jesus did not refer to the tithe as one of the "weightier provisions of the law." He did not mean by this that it is unimportant to be faithful in giving the tithe. It may be that He was saying what a church member said to me one time: "Giving my money to God is the easiest thing God calls on me to do. Anybody can write a check. That's not difficult. What is difficult to do is to live out faithfully the qualities of the Christian life and to be like our missionaries who have gone across the world to give

> **"Giving my money to God is the easiest thing God calls on me to do."**

their lives and the lives of their children to God. No, I would have to say that giving my money is the easiest thing anybody has ever asked me to do for God."

Jesus did not come to do away with the tithe or any part of the law. He came to fulfill the law. "Do not think that I came to abolish the Law or the Prophets; I did not come to abolish, but to fulfill" (Matthew 5:17 NASB).

Other Scriptural principles that are important to remember would include Haggai 2:8 KJV tells us that all money belongs to God: "The silver is mine, and the gold is mine, saith the Lord of Hosts."

1 Corinthians 4:7 NASB reminds us that all we have, we received from God. Therefore, we have no grounds for boasting about our possessions. "For who regards you as superior? And what do you have that you did not receive? But if you did receive it, why do you boast as if you had not received it?" Similarly, Deuteronomy 8:18 KJV points out that God is the One who gives us the ability to make money. "But thou shalt remember the Lord thy God: for it is he that giveth thee power to get wealth...."

Paul gives practical instruction regarding material gain in 1 Timothy 6:6-10. In verse 6, Paul teaches that we are to be content with what we have. Verse 7 reminds us that we came into the world with nothing, and we will leave this world with nothing. That truth should clearly illustrate to any reasonable person that our possessions upon earth are loaned to us while we are here. We are to be good stewards of what we receive, because it all belongs to God. Returning at least one-tenth to Him as He has commanded should be a minimum level of commitment for the Christian. The strong implication of the New Testament is that one-tenth is merely the starting place for all that grace requires.

Paul continues in verse 9 to point out that those who want to get rich are often plunged into foolish desires and ultimately into ruin and destruction. Verse 10, a well-known verse, reminds us it is the love of money that is the root of all sorts of evil. Notice that he does not say, as some have misquoted, that money is the root of all sorts of evil. It is not an evil thing to have wealth as long as the person who has been blessed in this way is faithful to the Lord with his or her possessions.

In 1 Corinthians 16:2, Paul teaches that the first day of the week is the appropriate time to set aside the offering for the Lord. The first day of the week was the day of worship for believers following the resurrection of Christ, which took place on the first day of the week. In this way, believers today bring their tithes and offerings on Sunday, the first day of the week, to set that money aside for the Lord and His work. Doing so is a meaningful act of worship especially as we consider how God has richly blessed our lives.

My father told me an interesting story about his first church. When he was meeting with the pulpit committee, one of the men on the committee said, "Brother White, I serve as the treasurer for the church, and I have a question. I am assuming that you will tithe your income from our church?" Dad responded that he most certainly would tithe. The treasurer then said, "Well, since you are a tither, and I was sure you would be, we will just deduct your ten percent for the church when we give you your paycheck. That way we will be able to cut back on the paperwork of your having to fill out a check and give the money right back to us." Dad remembered how surprised he was at the suggestion. He said, "No way am I going to let you do that. I don't want to miss the joyful experience of being able to give my tithe to the Lord as an act of worship."

I can certainly understand his response. For me, the morning offering time is one of the most exciting moments in the worship service when I have the opportunity to return to the Lord some of the blessings that He has poured out upon our lives. Also, I am sure you have heard this before, and I believe it to be true, you can never out-give God. God will not allow you to suffer loss because you faithfully give the tithe to Him. Of course, you do need to handle the balance of your finances in a responsible manner. When you are faithful and responsible, God will bless you beyond measure. He has

When you are faithful and responsible, God will bless you beyond measure.

promised to do so: "Give, and it will be given to you; good measure, pressed down, shaken together, running over, they will pour into your lap. For whatever measure you deal out to others, it will be dealt to you in return" (Luke 6:38 NASB). This is not prosperity theology; this is Scripture. It is the promise of God. In fact, in the Malachi passage cited earlier, the Lord says, "...and prove me now herewith, saith the Lord of hosts..." (Malachi 3:10b KJV). God is challenging you to put Him to the test and see if He will not pour out upon your life a blessing that is so great there will not be enough room to receive it.

2 Corinthians 8 is one of the Biblical texts on stewardship that has inspired me over the years. In this passage, Paul is commending the churches of Macedonia for their generosity in giving to the offering for the Jerusalem church. In verse two Paul says, "How that in a great trial of affliction the abundance of their joy and their deep poverty abounded unto the riches of their liberality" (2 Corinthians 8:2 KJV). Did you catch that? Out of "…the abundance of their joy…" they gave liberally to the offering for the Jerusalem church. Their joy did not come because they gave to the offering. The joy was there before they gave. Their joy was not the result of having plenty to give. They were impoverished. So, where did the joy come from? Verse 5 holds the answer to that question: "And this they did, not as we hoped, but first gave their own selves to the Lord, and unto us by the will of God" (2 Corinthians 8:5 KJV).

When you give your life to the Lord, it answers a thousand other questions for you.

Their joy and their generosity came from the fact that they had already given themselves to the Lord. When you give your life to the Lord, it answers a thousand other questions for you. You don't have to ask yourself every Sunday morning, "Should I go to church today, or stay at home?" You don't have to ask, "Will I tithe my income to the Lord, or can I just throw a few dollars in the offering plate?" "Will I serve the Lord through my church, or just sit back and let others do the work?" When you give your life to the Lord first, these and many other questions are answered for you. Accepting Jesus Christ as your Savior and Lord involves not only acceptance, but also the commitment of your life to Him. The commitment of life involves all of your life, not just your Sunday morning life. It involves all of your possessions, not just the tithe. It involves all of your time, not just an hour or two a week. When you give Christ your life, the rewards are greater than the costs. One of the greatest rewards is joy. That's why cheerful stewardship is not only possible, nothing else makes sense.

A circus athlete made his living by displaying remarkable feats of physical strength. His show would normally conclude with a simple, but impressive, demonstration of his ability to squeeze an orange dry. After completing his act, he would then challenge his audience to produce anyone who could extract even one drop of juice from the crushed fruit. On one such occasion as he challenged the audience, a rather small fellow at the back of the crowd volunteered to give it a try. The performer brought the man up on the platform and handed him the crushed orange. The little fellow rolled up his sleeve and took the orange in his hand. He began to squeeze the orange with all of his might. In a few moments, a small bit of juice began to form on the lower edge of the orange, and then a drop appeared. The drop fell from the orange to the platform and the audience exploded into cheers and applause. After the cheers subsided, the athlete asked the man's name and invited him to tell everyone how he had managed to develop such fistic powers. "Nothing to it," replied the man. Then with a grin he added, "I happen to be the treasurer of the Baptist church in our community."

This church treasurer's expertise is not needed in a healthy church, where cheerful stewardship is the norm, and the members of the church have first given themselves to God. For them, giving is an act of worship filled with joy.

QUALITY #8: ON MISSION FOR CHRIST

*I*t was during the 1970's, when I was serving as pastor of the Tabernacle Baptist Church in Carrollton, Georgia, that I attended an associational Brotherhood meeting at First Baptist Church of Carrollton. Eugene Dailey, director of the Brotherhood Department for the Georgia Baptist Convention, was our guest speaker for the evening. Gene began to talk about how the men in our churches needed to be challenged to become involved in hands-on mission work. I remember his commenting that their involvement in missions would change their lives and have a tremendous impact upon our churches.

Gene was well ahead of the curve in his message that night. It would be two to three decades before volunteer missions would really catch on among Southern Baptist churches. Gene told about a mission project that needed the assistance of some men with building expertise. He spoke of the Grace Baptist Church in Greenwood, Indiana, on the outskirts of Indianapolis. He talked about the strong leadership of the pastor, Charles Smith, and how the church was now meeting in the clubhouse of a country club. They had reached the point of outgrowing that space and needed a church building. He laid the vision before us that evening of how someone from the Carrollton Baptist Association could take a team of workers and go to Indiana and build that church. Then Gene looked right at me. I'll never forget it. He looked right at me and said, "Bob, you have enough men in your church that if you all wanted to, you could take a team of builders up there and build that church. I want you to think about doing that."

I did think about it. I thought about it constantly. I couldn't get it off of my mind or heart. I prayed that the Lord would let me know clearly if this was what He wanted us to do. This would be a brand new venture for our church, never having been on a mission trip before. The Lord would not allow me to escape the sense of calling I had for this special project. I went by the home of W.O. and Irene Kilgore, two of our fine lay people, to discuss the possibility. Wenton was a fine builder with years and years of experience. He said, "Pastor, if you believe that God would have us to attempt something like this, I will do everything I can to make it happen." Wenton and Irene both got excited. I asked if he would be willing to be on site for the project, explaining that it would take weeks. He responded enthusiastically that they would take their Airstream trailer to Indiana and park it on the site and operate from there. He suggested that we to talk to Phil McGukin, a young residential builder in our church, about taking one of his framing crews to the church to

This would be a brand new venture for our church, never having been on a mission trip before.

frame the building. Wenton said, "Preacher, if you get a bunch of amateurs to go up there and frame that building, nothing will be square, and finishing the project will be much more difficult."

I talked to Phil about this mission opportunity, and he got excited. He committed his framing crew to the project. We set a starting date, and we were on our way. The project was an incredible success. We used a simple design that had been produced by the Architecture Department of the Southern Baptist Sunday School Board.

The framing was completed within one week. It was time for me to get involved. I was one of the amateurs that Wenton had referred to. I went to the hardware store and bought a nail apron and got my hammer and a seven-inch circular saw. I was ready for anything that might come my way, or so I thought. When I got to Greenwood, it was time to put the roofing paper on the building. "No problem," I said. "I can do that." Wenton said, "Preacher, have you ever done any work on a roof?" "Oh, sure," I said, "many times." I remembered that I did go up on the roof of the house a couple of times as a kid when I got my ball or glider plane stuck up there. I really was not prepared for the work that was coming my way. It was July, so we began working about 6:30 in the morning to take advantage of the cooler temperatures. By 10:00 o'clock, it was so hot on that roof that I thought I would die. That roofing paper gets slippery as butter when the temperature on the roof gets around 100 degrees. I tried to do

That roofing paper gets slippery as butter when the temperature on the roof gets around 100 degrees.

my part, but I had to come down the ladder for a water break and to cool down quite a few times. I wanted to say, "I believe I'll just help the ladies prepare the pimiento cheese sandwiches," but I didn't dare.

After all the work was done, the pastor invited me to preach the dedication sermon. What a thrill it was to stand in the pulpit of the church that our people built with their own hands. That day God blessed me with a wonderful surprise. My cousin, Bill, who was not a Christian and lived in Indianapolis, came to hear me preach and was saved in the worship service.

Later I had an opportunity to go to Hong Kong on a preaching mission. John Bisagno preached in the football stadium at night and about 30 of us pastors would witness in the streets during the day and preach in the churches on Sunday. It was the thrill of a lifetime. We saw around 4,000 salvations in ten days. The experiences from those ten days punctuated my preaching for years.

While pastoring in Kentucky, I took a team of laity from our church on a partnership mission trip to Kenya. I preached in the bush and in the villages. The public address system ran off of the truck battery. Tommy McIntosh, a great Christian layman and a builder and general specialist in anything that has to do with building, was in charge of wiring the system at each stop. He and others on the trip were seasoned witnesses for Christ. I remember someone approaching me before we left for Kenya to ask the age-old question: "Why are you going halfway around the world when we have plenty of people around here who need saving?" I told this person a story. "My Dad and I used to fish quite a bit together. It was our favorite thing to do. There were times that we would go and fish all day with only one or two bites and no catch. Every now and then, someone would say that they really got into the fish at such and such location on the lake. Dad would find out exactly how to get there so we could also get into some good fishing. Well, we have been told that the fishing is great in Kenya. Hundreds of thousands are responding to the Gospel, and Jesus has commanded us to be fishers of men. So, we're going to Kenya, because I have heard that the fishing is really good over there."

Indeed, the fishing was good. Eight of us preached and shared the Gospel for ten days and saw 1,000 new believers coming to faith in Christ! While there, I had the privilege of baptizing seven new believers at the edge of a village of thatched huts. The members of the church gathered around the banks of the stream and sang as the baptismal candidates walked one-by-one down into the water. They would stop singing while the person was being

I had the privilege of baptizing seven new believers at the edge of a village of thatched huts.

baptized. Then as soon as I raised the new believer out of the water, they would break into the most joyful singing I had ever heard. It was a glorious experience.

There have been mission trips to Germany, South America, South Korea, France and other places. Through each experience, God has deepened my personal commitment to Him and to the importance of missions. I have consistently returned from these experiences, as have those with me, with a renewed and strengthened commitment to the Cooperative Program and our mission offerings which provide support to our missionaries around the world. There is no finer group of people in the world today than our Southern Baptist missionaries. Many of them are living at the edge of peril on a constant basis. They have sacrificed the comforts of America to share Christ with those who are lost. They are the embodiment of The Great Commission of Christ to "Go therefore and make disciples of all the nations, baptizing them in the name of the Father and the Son and the Holy Spirit, teaching them to observe all that I commanded you; and lo, I am with you always, even to the end of the age" (Matthew 28:19-20 NASB).

On March 25–27, 1998, the Georgia Baptist Convention sponsored our first "President's Cooperative Program Summit." The goal of the summit was to discover what we need to do to assure the continued strength of the Cooperative Program into the 21st Century. Two hundred thirty-nine people from our churches, associations, and institutions participated in the Summit. They were young and old. They were men and women. They were ministers and laity. All agreed that for missions giving to remain strong in the new century, we must have increased involvement in volunteer missions. It was concluded that, whereas there was a time when our people were willing to send their mission money to Southern Baptist causes with very little personal involvement in missions, this has largely changed. Now, people like to see where their money is going. They like

Now, people like to see where their money is going.

to get involved and touch missions one-on-one. I believe that makes this a great day for Southern Baptist missions. Our missionaries have invited increased involvement for decades, and finally we are catching on.

The President's Cooperative Program Summit reported to the Convention in the fall of 1998 that there needs to be more personalization of missions. The report made several strong points regarding involvement of Georgia Baptists in missions:

- It is imperative that churches be offered a more intimately involved connection with mission work. As one person stated it, "The Cooperative Program needs a face."

- There must be further efforts made to involve all Georgia Baptists in actual mission endeavors. Ministry resource consultants as well as associational missionaries need to develop a strategy of gathering small churches into task forces to do mission trips on state, national and international levels. It would be helpful to encourage and highlight model churches that are doing this as an encouragement to others.

- Since pastors are the key to church involvement and often individual involvement in missions work, there needs to be a much greater effort on the part of the International Mission Board, North American Mission Board, Georgia Baptist Convention and local associations to involve pastors in actual hands-on mission work at each level. There must be personal involvement that is initiated by one-on-one invitation by mission board personnel.[1]

Last year, our state convention sent nearly 150,000 people out on volunteer mission projects. These are short-term projects based on needs expressed by our missionaries. Our Mission Volunteers Department receives mission project requests from the missionaries and then matches those requests with mission teams from our state who have indicated that they are prepared to go. Those who participate in the mission trip are responsible for their own expenses,

A more involved congregation is a happier and healthier congregation.

and in many cases, these persons have to take time off from work in order to be a part of the mission trip. Inevitably, participants return with a new fire in their hearts for missions. Their prayers for the missionaries take on new significance, and their gifts to missions are more generous and meaningful. These short-term mission volunteers become proponents for the mission exper-ience, and they enlist the interest of more and more church members. The outcome of all of this is predictable. A more involved congregation is a happier and healthier congregation.

The numbers of persons in recent years who have wanted to be involved in mission projects has led us to increase the number of our mission partnerships. We used to have one international and one North American

---

1 *Book of Minutes*, "President's Cooperative Program Summit," (Georgia Baptist Convention, Atlanta, Georgia 1998), p. 42.

mission partnership. Our thinking was that we should not assume too many partnerships at one time lest we find ourselves unable to provide ample involvement and support for the partnerships. We reached a point, however, where there were so many Georgia Baptists wanting to go on mission trips that our partners had to say, "We can't take anymore volunteers. There are more of you than there are of us, and we simply cannot accommodate all who wish to come." We were both surprised and excited about this challenge. New partnerships were added. At this writing, we are in mission partnerships with the cities of Rochester and Buffalo, New York, and San Diego, California. We are in partnership with the state conventions of Utah/Idaho and California. Currently, talks are underway with the Baptist Convention of New York to consider partnering with the State of New York with a special focus on New York City. The aftermath of the September 11th attacks on the World Trade Center has created a tremendous need in New York as well as a unique openness to the Gospel of Christ. Internationally, we are in partnership with the nations of France and Moldova. It has been remarkable to see the expansion of our mission partnership ministry. It has grown rapidly and appears that it will continue to grow as more and more people engage in volunteer mission projects.

Not only did Jesus speak clearly the mandate to missions in The Great Commission of Matthew 28, He extended that mandate with a promise of power for the believer in Acts 1:8 KJV: "But ye shall receive power, after that the Holy Ghost is come upon you: and ye shall be witnesses unto me both in Jerusalem, and in all Judea, and in Samaria, and unto the uttermost part of the earth."

From the preceding verses, it is evident that the disciples were distracted from their mission by their concerns for the future of Israel. Jesus said, "It is not for you to know the times or the seasons, which the Father hath put in his own power" (Acts 1:7 KJV). Then with one word, the conjunction "but," Jesus turned the disciples around and sent them in the right direction. "But you shall receive power after the Holy Ghost has come upon you." The miraculous power of the Holy Spirit lives in the life of every believer. There is, therefore, nothing that God will ask you to do that you will be unable to accomplish. This is wonderful news for the Christian. Jesus, speaking of the Holy Spirit in John 14 said:

The miraculous power of the Holy Spirit lives in the life of every believer.

> "And I will pray the Father, and he shall give you another Comforter, that he may abide with you forever; Even the Spirit of truth; whom the world cannot receive, because it seeth him not, neither knoweth him: but ye know him; for he dwelleth with you, and shall be in you. I will not leave you comfortless: I will come to you. Yet a little while, and the world seeth me no more; but ye see me: because I live, ye shall live also. At that day ye shall know that I am in my Father, and ye in me, and I in you."
> *(John 14:16-20 KJV)*

When you made your commitment to Christ, He really did take up residence in your life. Jesus described the Comforter, the Holy Spirit, in the third person in verses 16-17. Then in verses 18-20, Jesus speaks of the Holy Spirit in the first person, "I will not leave you comfortless: I will come to you."

A little boy who had just given his life to Jesus on Sunday evening was discovered by his mother sitting at the breakfast table on Monday morning with his hand on his chest feeling the beat, beat, beat of his heart. Excitedly, he said, "Mom, I really do have Jesus in my heart. I feel Him bumping around in there." There is no greater power afforded the Christian than to have Jesus in his or her heart.

Then Jesus said, "You shall be my missionaries." "No," you say. "That's not what the verse says. It says 'You shall be my witnesses.'" Yes, you're right, but what is a missionary? A missionary is one who is a witness, a witness to the power and glory of the resurrected Jesus Christ. We are to be His witnesses, His missionaries. You might say, "I know who the missionaries are. They are those wonderful folks who are serving in Africa, South America, Australia, Europe, and Asia. They are the ones who are preaching and teaching the

> **A missionary is one who is a witness, a witness to the power and glory of the resurrected Jesus Christ.**

Gospel in the international cities and villages throughout the world." Yes they are, but remember that a lost person in your town or city is just as lost as that lost person in Nairobi or Sydney or Hong Kong or Frankfort or Rio. It's an amazing thing that we will go across the world to be a missionary, but we won't go next door, or across the street. Is that lost person next door to you any less valuable to God than the lost person in Calcutta?

I like the story about the man who believed that God was calling his sister to be a missionary. Faithfully he prayed for her, "Lord, I know that you are calling my sister to be a missionary. I pray that she will hear Your call and respond to Your will." Then one day God surprised him. While he was praying about his sister, God called him to be a missionary. The world is full of people who are praying "Here am I, Lord; send my sister. Here am I, Lord; send my brother," when what God really wants is you. He wants you to be His missionary. It might be right where you live, or across the world.

Then Jesus gave the disciples, and us, the geography of our mission. We are to carry the Gospel to our Jerusalem, Judea, Samaria, and to the uttermost part of the earth. Would you be willing to make a commitment to be an Acts 1:8 Christian? In making that commitment you are saying that you will be on mission in your Jerusalem, your town or city. You will be on mission in your Judea, your state. You will be on mission in your Samaria, your nation. You will be on mission to the uttermost, your world. Would your church be an Acts 1:8 church? Would your association be an Acts 1:8 association? Would your state convention be an Acts 1:8 state convention? Wouldn't it be great if there was that kind of response to the clear mandate of Acts 1:8?

One of our associations, the Columbus Baptist Association in Columbus, Georgia, informed me that they had already made the commitment to be an Acts 1:8 association. Their plan for this year is to have people from the association on mission in Jerusalem, Judea, Samaria, and to the uttermost. What a wonderful commitment and what a great example this is to all of us. I heard recently of a church that made the commitment that the sun would never set on their mission work. In other words, they would have people from their church serving simultaneously around the world in such a way that the sun would always be shining on their church's mission ministry. That is a powerful witness! That is a healthy church!

I heard recently of a church that made the commitment that the sun would never set on their mission work.

When I took the team of eight mission volunteers from our church in Kentucky to Kenya, we did a lot of work, a lot of witnessing, and from time to time, we laughed over the hilarious things that always happen in international travel. I remember one afternoon we arrived at a field where we would have a worship service. While Tommy McIntosh was hooking up the amplifier to the truck battery, a group of people walked up to one of our senior adult volunteers whose name was Charles Henn. One of the Kenyans, I suppose because of our very white skin, asked, "Are you Finnish [from Finland]?" Charles responded: "No, we haven't started yet."

When I think about the future of our witness, our call, to proclaim Christ to the world, I trust that we can all agree that we are not finished; we are just getting started.

With healthy Kingdom churches focused on being missionaries to our Jerusalem, Judea, Samaria and the uttermost, the best is yet to be.

⊠

QUALITY #9: A GOOD REPUTATION IN THE COMMUNITY

A little boy was standing on a front porch on tiptoe trying as hard as he could to reach the doorbell. A lady who happened to be walking by on the sidewalk saw what was happening and went up on the porch to help the little boy. She picked him up so that he could reach the bell. He rang the bell several times. The lady, still holding the little boy said, "What now?" The boy responded, "Lady, run like crazy!"

Now, that's not a particularly good way to win friends and influence your neighbors. Some churches, however, have very effectively used the ringing of doorbells to build their relationship with the community. Just ask Robert Schuller. A few years ago, I heard him tell how he started the Garden Grove Community Church in Orange County, California. He said: "I knew that no great church could be built without being in touch with the community. I wanted to discover what the needs of the community might be and how our new congregation would be able to meet those needs. So, when I started the church, I literally went door to door asking a single question. 'What can the Garden Grove Community Church do for you?' Every time, that question was answered, I made note of the response. It was upon that information from the community that I built the ministry of our church."

People argue that it is no longer good methodology to ring doorbells. Some churches contact their community in this way with great success; others find different ways to get their message across. The key is to demonstrate sincere interest in the people of your community. Learn what the needs of the community are, and then respond by meeting those needs.

One pastor told me that he discovered a need in the community high school. They needed help with the concession stand during football games on Friday evenings. The Booster Club parents wanted to see their kids play ball and perform at halftime. The pastor said, "Our church will take care of that for you," and they did. You can imagine the goodwill that built in the community for the church. An association said, "We were convicted following the tragedies of 9/11 that we had not been expressive of our gratitude for our policemen, firemen and EMT folks in our community. We want to plan a major event to demonstrate to them how much we appreciate what they do for us everyday." Another congregation turns their property into the village of Bethlehem every Christmas season with remarkably artistic shops and city streets. They have live animals and hundreds of church members dressed in costume. Through this method, they share the message of Christ with

In hundreds of ways, churches are making attempts to build good will in their communities and through these open doors to share the Gospel of Christ.

their community. They said, "We see it as our gift to the community at Christmastime." Other churches provide seasonal dramas or concerts of spiritual music in the open air, in the civic concert hall, or in their church worship center. In hundreds of ways, churches are making attempts to build good will in their communities and through these open doors to share the Gospel of Christ.

In Acts we read about the early church "Praising God, and having favor with all the people" (Acts 2:47a KJV). In other words, they enjoyed a wonderful reputation in the community. Now, if you want to talk about a tough time in history to be the church, this first century church was living in a time when people were being slaughtered simply because it was discovered that they were Christians. I'm sure they would have loved to be able to say that their biggest problem was concern over the ringing of doorbells and whether that was an acceptable method.

> **Can you imagine how glorious it would be to witness the baptism of 3,000 new believers in one day?**

The church was obviously highly successful in reaching their community for Christ. Verse 41 of Acts 2 KJV says, "Then they that gladly received his word were baptized: and the same day there were added unto them about three thousand souls." What a wonderful baptismal service that was. Can you imagine how glorious it would be to witness the baptism of 3,000 new believers in one day?

The church, in fact, was growing by leaps and bounds during one of the most difficult times in history. In Acts

1:15, the church had 120 members; in Acts 2:41, there were 3,000 believers added to the church in one day. Acts 2:47 says that people were being added to the church daily. How wonderful it would be to have baptism in your church every day of the week because the church was growing so rapidly it was difficult to keep up with the baptisms. Acts 4:4 reports that 5,000 men were added to the church in one day. Acts 5:14 says that multitudes of believers, both men and women, were added to the church. In Acts 6:1 and 7, it says that the number of believers multiplied. Now the church was experiencing not only addition, but also multiplication.

How was it that this remarkable growth took place? No doubt God's hand was upon the church, but what was the church doing right? As you know, it is possible to get in God's way and thwart His will by our disobedience and unfaithfulness to His Word. The church in Acts was certainly not shy about boldly presenting the Gospel of Jesus Christ. I heard a teenage girl give her testimony on television the other night. She used a phrase that I had heard before, "If you don't stand for something, you will fall for anything." The church in the Book of Acts was on fire for Christ. There was no question in their community about who they were or what they stood for. I believe that herein lies a real key to having a good reputation in the community. People today need to see someone who will stand for something. There are plenty of people who are falling for anything. The greatest strength of the church's reputation will be built upon faithfulness to who we are. This includes our faithfulness to the truths of the Bible, our faithfulness to the lordship of Jesus Christ, our unswerving commitment to be the church, standing for what is right.

Your reputation is built upon your faithfulness to who you are. When the church tries to be something other than the church, it loses credibility with the community. For example, political correctness is the order of the day. Political correctness, however, is not necessarily compatible with God's Word. For the church there should never be a discussion over which is more important—to be politically correct, or to be Biblically sound. When political correctness is in conflict with the Bible, the church should come down on the side of the Bible every time. I'm talking about 100% of the time, not 98% or 99% of the time, but 100% of the time.

> **When political correctness is in conflict with the Bible, the church should come down on the side of the Bible every time.**

Our state Convention had to take a strong stand on the issue of homosexuality a few years ago. Publicly, we affirmed that we love the homosexual, but do not approve of and cannot condone the sin of homosexuality. We challenged all of our churches to minister to homosexuals, but to be honest with homosexuals about their need to repent and turn to Christ. There were some people within the Convention who wanted a softer stance. The radio talk show hosts and the newspapers had a field day with the matter. Numerous persons complained that this was bad public relations for the Convention. In making an assessment like that, one needs to consider that the media in this country is, generally speaking, liberal in its views. There is tremendous power in the media to sway public opinion, and it is used with regularity to attack the church. Even Baptists are guilty of attributing too much credibility to what they hear on radio and television or read in the paper. We are not to establish our position on the changing tides of public opinion. Before we speak to critical issues that impact the moral fiber of our community, are we supposed to put our finger in the air to check wind direction first? I want to suggest to you that, if we do, we are endangering our reputation as the people of God. The church, association, convention or other Christian body that consistently checks to see which way the wind is blowing before it takes a stand on Biblical truths has sacrificed its position of spiritual leadership in the community, and rightly so.

During the challenging days following the Convention's stand, while I received some negative letters from Baptists, the overwhelming number of letters and calls I received from Baptists were supportive of the stand. I thought it particularly interesting that I received many words of encouragement from Methodists, Presbyterians, and Catholics. They were saying, "Thank you for taking a stand for Biblical morality." One Saturday I was helping my son-in-law at his sandwich shop when I met a nice Methodist couple. When they discovered that I was with the Georgia Baptist Convention, they said, "We want to thank you for the strong stand you all took on the homosexual issue. We have been saddened by other denominations which have not done the right thing in standing upon God's Word on this matter. We say, thank the Lord for the Baptists!" A banker in Decatur told one of our fine laymen how much he appreciated the fact that Georgia Baptists were willing to do the right thing rather than follow the lines of least resistance.

What is the community looking for from its churches? I believe the answer to that question is conviction and consistency, not compatibility. Without fail, we should proclaim the truth in love. Without compromise we should uphold the Word of God. Without hesitancy we should be who we are. A good reputation in the community comes not from making people feel good,

> **Without compromise we should uphold the Word of God.**

but in helping people to know good, do good and be good. A good reputation in the community comes from being the church that Jesus Christ established us to be, a church of believers who declare with deep conviction, "Thou art the Christ, the Son of the living God" (Matthew 16:16 KJV).

At the conclusion of 2001, survey results from the Gallup Poll, the Gallup Organization, or the Gallup Youth Survey reported the following facts:

- "Morality, ethics and dishonesty" are named as the top problem facing the nation, for only the second time in a half-century.

- Biblical literalism, the belief that the Bible represents the actual Word of God in all instances, has declined over the last few decades, and is now at the lowest point ever recorded, 27%.

- Fifty-four percent of U.S. adults are not opposed to hiring homosexuals for the clergy.

- Religion is gaining ground, but morality is losing ground. Churchgoing, Bible reading, belief in Heaven and Hell, as well as other religious beliefs and practices, show gains. At the same time, however, a solid majority of the public believes that religion is losing its influence on American life.[1]

There can be no doubt, it is time for the church to stand up and be counted as faithful. The reputation of the church takes a significant hit every time the church exhibits worldly practices. It may be a Baptist pastor who has fallen, or a Catholic priest. The reputation is weakened by failure in any quarter. We all suffer when one falls regardless of the denomination. Why is this so? It is so because it represents inconsistency with who we are as the church. Stay the course, church. Follow the Lord and stay the course.

Stay the course, church. Follow the Lord and stay the course.

A few years ago I had a wonderful opportunity to learn to fly. I was a pastor in Carrollton, Georgia, at the time. One of our fine laymen, Joe Whit Walker, purchased a Cessna 150 for his son to begin flying lessons. Joe was gracious in allowing me to use the plane. My flight instructor was Bob Husby, who was an incredible pilot.

1 "Emerging Trends." Princeton Religion Research Center, Vol. 23, No. 9, December 2001, p.1.

His instincts as a pilot were strong, and he imparted his knowledge and experience to me. I'll never forget his cautioning me about flying at night. He said, "Whenever you fly, day or night, take a flashlight with you, because, even if you take off in daylight, you may be later getting back than you expected, and you need to have a flashlight in case you lose the lighting on your instrument panel."

Then he said, "Let me tell you a story about the kind of flashlight you need to take with you. I had a student who got his license and to celebrate took his wife and another couple in a Cessna to Panama City, Florida, for a seafood dinner. He had his flashlight with him. He used the light for his preflight check of the exterior of the airplane. Then when he got in the plane, he put the light on top of his instrument panel. They took off, headed for Panama City. They were having a great time talking, laughing and visiting with each other. He was not paying attention to what was happening. As he approached two hours into the flight, he realized that it should have taken him only one hour and forty minutes. He couldn't see the lights of Panama City, or any other city for that matter. He was surrounded by total darkness. He strained his eyes as he looked out his side window and then broke into a cold sweat. All he could see was water below him. He was out over the Gulf of Mexico and had no idea which direction was land. He quickly tried to evaluate his problem and why his instruments had failed. It was then that he discovered that the flashlight he used was one of those that has a magnet on it. He had put it in the worst possible place—on top of his instrument cluster. The magnet had drawn the compass and every other instrument off course. He was fortunate because, when he removed the flashlight, the instruments all returned to proper readings. Whatever you do, don't take a flashlight that has a magnet on it."

As the church, we must be careful about being drawn off course. There are many distractions in the world today and there are powerful influences which could draw us off course if we lose our true North heading.

> **As the church, we must be careful about being drawn off course.**

The church must be true to give to the community that which no one else gives. There are civic groups that provide services to the community. There are charities that provide aid to the downtrodden. Police and fire units provide help to the distressed. EMT's provide emergency medical care. Hospitals and nursing homes provide short-term and long-term care. Relief agencies provide food and clothing. Government agencies provide care for the indigent, for neglected and abused children. The church is also involved in many of these ministries to the community, and that is good, but the church is called to provide something that no one else provides. The church provides the Gospel of Jesus Christ to a world that is hungering and thirsting for the food that gives eternal life.

In John 6, Jesus referred to Himself as The Bread of Life Who came from heaven to provide food and drink to those who believe so that they will never hunger or thirst again (John 6:35). He went on to say that eternal life comes to those who eat of His flesh and drink of His blood (John 6:54). Those who heard Jesus speak in the synagogue at

Capernaum on this occasion said, "This is a difficult statement; who can listen to it?" (John 6:60b NASB).

Jesus was speaking of His approaching death on the cross and the cost of discipleship for those who would follow Him. Jesus knew that this was difficult for His followers to hear. He also knew this was a time of sifting when those who had been following Him for the wrong reasons needed to make their exit. Many followed Him because they had been among the multitude when Jesus fed them with the loaves and fish. Because of this great miracle, they had wanted to make Him their king. They did not understand the mission of Christ. After many went away from following Jesus, He turned to His twelve disciples and said, "You do not want to go away also, do you? Simon Peter answered Him, 'Lord, to whom shall we go? You have words of eternal life. And we have believed and have come to know that You are the Holy One of God'" (John 6:67-69 NASB).

There are some very significant points to be discovered in Peter's words. First of all, the disciples acknowledged that there was a need to have someone that they could go to with the deep concerns and needs of their lives. Second, they knew of no one else to whom they might turn to have their needs met. Should they turn back to the prophets of old who had lived and died. These prophets had spent their entire ministries pointing to the coming of another. Should they turn to the teachers, the Rabbis of their day? Their message did not satisfy the heart as did the message of Jesus. "For he taught them as one having authority, and not as the scribes" (Matthew 7:29 KJV). Third, the disciples knew that Jesus had what they needed—words of eternal life. Nothing else really mattered. Why should they turn to any other person? Jesus was the One Who possessed the words of eternal life.

There is a clear parallel which can be drawn for the church's relationship to the community. There is a basic need among all people everywhere, particularly in these troubling times, to have someone they can turn to for comfort, peace, assurance, guidance, wisdom, and most importantly, the promise of eternal life. We know that person is Jesus Christ. We also know that the church is the only institution in the world today with the responsibility of pointing people to Christ. The church that becomes involved in all kinds of social ministry and does great work in caring for the physical and emotional needs of those in the community, but fails to boldly preach the Gospel of Jesus Christ,

> **It is time for the church to be the church and declare with conviction that people without Christ are lost.**

has seriously misjudged its responsibility and ultimately damaged its reputation in the community. There are basic spiritual needs in every person that need to be met. In John 6, Jesus was saying, if all you want from Me is food, you will need to get satisfied somewhere else. My gaze is set upon the cross and if you wish to follow Me, you must be prepared to partake in My suffering.

It is time for the church to be the church and declare with conviction that people without Christ are lost. Faith in Christ is the only way to be saved; there is no other. Those who choose sin over faith in Christ and obedience to His Word are eternally doomed. Jesus the Christ is the only One Who has the words of eternal life. Say it church! People are lost without Christ. Say it! "But wait a minute, if we say that, we are going to hurt someone's feelings. You know, everybody doesn't believe the way we do. You can't just up and tell people that they are going to hell without Christ. That may have been well and good in the 1950's, but we are in the 21st Century, and we no longer believe in absolutes. There are many ways to heaven." Is that right? Where in the Bible does it say there are many ways to heaven? "Well, it may not be in the Bible, but I heard them talking about this on a talk show the other evening on television, and they clearly said that people just don't believe that anymore." So what? Is the Word of God changed by the opinions of persons who have not believed in Jesus as the Christ? "He that believeth on him is not condemned: but he that believeth not is condemned already, because he hath not believed in the name of the only begotten Son of God" (John 3:18 KJV). Persons who posit the philosophy that Jesus is not the only way to be saved are condemned. Are you going to take the word of a condemned man over the Word of God? Not this Christian, not now, not ever!

The church can perform many ministries to develop a good reputation in the community. Such ministry is commendable for many reasons, but its aim should be for the ultimate purpose of opening the heart of the community to receive the message of the church. The one thing the church must do, as the church in Acts did faithfully, is to preach the truth about Jesus.

QUALITY #10: PEOPLE BEING ADDED TO THE CHURCH

*O*n a visit to one of our churches recently, I noticed that the baptistry was filled with water. I asked the pastor if he would be having a baptism in the morning worship service. He said, "No, not this morning. We keep the baptistry filled in anticipation of the next person who is going to be saved. We don't want our baptistry to ever dry up."

Contrast that with a visit to another church where the pastor was showing me through the church facility. When we came to the baptistry area, I looked in and saw that the baptistry had become a storage area where old boxes of materials had been stored. Flower vases, vacuum cleaner, wooden podiums, and other unused items were crowded into the baptistry. I didn't say anything about it, but my heart was saddened by this church which would have to have a garage sale in order to have a baptism. A church that is winning people to Jesus and adding people to the church is a healthy church. A church that never wins anyone to Christ is not a healthy church. Did you say, "never wins anyone to Christ?" I surely did. It is sad to say, but we have congregations in our Convention, who have not won anyone to Christ in years. In the year 2001 there were 556 churches in the Georgia Baptist Convention that did not baptize one person. That is difficult to

In the year 2001 there were 556 churches in the Georgia Baptist Convention that did not baptize one person.

understand when you realize that some folks refer to our area of the country as the buckle on the Bible Belt.

The early church in the Book of Acts went about actively preaching the Gospel of Christ. As a result, many were coming to faith in Christ everyday. Acts 2:47b NASB reports: "And the Lord was adding to their number day by day those who were being saved."

Some would argue, "Okay, you are in Atlanta where you have a witnessing pool of 4,000,000 people. We live in a largely rural county with a small population. It's not as easy for us to locate lost people who haven't already been contacted 15 times by every church in the county." I do understand that. But no place is without lost people. With approximately 60 percent of our state being unchurched, there is always a harvest in the field. Besides, who says you can't contact that family again, even if they have been contacted 15 times before. The next time might be the occasion when they come to Christ.

I preached a revival in West Georgia at the Flat Rock Baptist Church. The pastor, Ronnie Puckett, said, "I'd like for us to go to the home of one of my church members to visit her husband who has never made a profession of faith." I told him that I would be glad to go with him on the visit. On the way out to the house, Ronnie told me that this dear lady had been praying for her husband for over 40 years. He was now in his 70s. Every year Ronnie would respond to the request of the wife to bring the evangelist by to share Christ with her husband. When we reached the home, the man was cutting the grass. He stopped the mower and greeted us warmly. He said that his wife was not there at the moment. The pastor said that was fine because we had come to talk with him. He was very polite and offered chairs for us to sit in out on the lawn.

After introductory conversation, I told this gentleman that I wanted to talk with him about trusting Jesus Christ as his Savior. We found his heart wide open. Within a few minutes, he was praying to receive Christ. You can imagine the joy of his faithful wife when she learned that he had given his life to the Lord. The entire church and community rejoiced over the news.

I am confident that I didn't share the faith any differently from every other evangelist that Ronnie had taken out to visit with this warm-hearted man. Many times he had rejected the witness; that day he prayed to receive Christ. How do you explain that? You don't. You just know that this is God's work, and often a visit is just a visit and at times, it is a divine appointment. Don't become discouraged when a visit appears to be nothing more than a visit, because God will use an individual to plant the seed of the Gospel in someone's heart, and others will water it. Then one day, God brings the increase. (1 Corinthians 3:6)

Attempting to reach the lost for Christ can be frustrating. It may mean that you go back to visit them multiple times. Don't ever stop going back to them. It may just be that next time, they will come to Christ.

Steve Parr, specialist of Bible Study Ministries for the Georgia Baptist Convention, would suggest that you get those prospects enrolled in Sunday School. If you can accomplish that, there is a high percentage of probability that they will eventually make their profession of faith, be baptized, and unite with the church. In a recent report, Steve addressed statements by Andy Anderson, a leader and prolific writer in Southern Baptist Sunday School ministry. Steve addressed Anderson's conclusions about Sunday School as an effective way to evangelize the lost. He did this by citing statistics from a 2001 study of the 50 fastest growing Sunday Schools among our 3,480 Georgia Baptist churches.

In his book, *The Growth Spiral*, Andy Anderson said that evangelism is best done through the Sunday School. He listed the following discoveries:

- The best methods for discovering evangelistic prospects are through the Sunday School.

- One-half of the people we enroll in Sunday School are unsaved.

- One out of two unsaved people whom we enroll in Sunday School will be saved and baptized in a year.

- After a person has been enrolled in Sunday School and then led to Christ, assimilation into the church membership is almost 100%.[1]

The 2001 study conducted by Bible Study Ministries revealed the 1.3% of Georgia Baptist Churches identified as the fastest growing accounted for 75% of the net gain in enrollment, and 42% of the net gain in attendance in Georgia above the previous year! In addition, these

---

1 Andy Anderson, *The Growth Spiral* (Nashville: Broadman and Holman Publishers, 1993), p. 128.

churches provided 15% of the total baptisms in the state for the same year. Some of the common factors of these Sunday Schools include practices such as the training of leaders, open enrollment, creation of new units, and the pastor's support of the Sunday School.[2]

In 2002, Bible Study Ministries has identified the top 100 fastest growing Sunday Schools. The criteria for the research included net growth in Sunday School attendance, percentage growth in Sunday School attendance, net growth in Sunday School enrollment, percentage growth in Sunday School enrollment, total baptisms, and baptism ratios. The information was taken from the Annual Church Profiles comparing the year 1998 to the year 2001. While many churches in the Convention are growing, these churches stand out as the best of the best.[3]

The study addressed Andy Anderson's assertions from 1993. The Annual Church Profiles of these churches were studied to determine the level of impact that their rapid growth had or did not have on cooperative missions giving and evangelism. Cooperative program giving and baptisms were compared for the years 1998 and 2001. Ninety-seven churches had information that was accessible at the time of the study. Those churches make up 2.7% of Georgia Baptist churches. In 2001, they accounted for 17.7% of the state's baptisms and 8.2% of the total Cooperative Program gifts. This is outstanding considering the fact that one-fourth of the churches average less than 100 in Sunday School attendance. The following chart summarizes the findings:[4]

---

2 Steve Parr, "The Impact of Sunday School Growth On Cooperative Missions Giving and Evangelism," Bible Study Ministries, Georgia Baptist Convention, Atlanta, Georgia, June 7, 2002. p. 1.

3 Ibid.

4 Ibid.

	1998 Baptisms	2001 Baptisms	Change
Top 25 Small SSs (<100)	110	360	+227%
Top 25 Intermediate SSs (100–199)	454	919	+102%
Top 25 Medium SSs (200–399)	873	1,448	+65%
Top 25 large SSs (400+)	3,009	3,710	+23%
Top 100 Growing SSs	**4,446**	**6,437**	**+45%**
All Georgia Baptist Convention Churches	**37,182**	**36,280**	**-2%**

Andy Anderson advocated and proved the impact of a growing Sunday School on evangelism and stewardship in the local church. The study affirms his findings and reinforces the importance of healthy Sunday Schools as they influence the local church, and on a broader scale, the state convention.[5]

Andy Anderson advocated and proved the impact of a growing Sunday School on evangelism and stewardship in the local church. The study affirms his findings.

Through whatever means we reach people for Christ and add them to the fellowship of the church, it can easily be said that seeing a person acknowledge Christ for the first time in their lives is the greatest thrill to be experienced by the church. Rarely have I ever seen people responding at invitation time that I did not see someone, and often quite a few people, weeping for joy. This is not just good for the new believer; this is good for the church.

5 Ibid., p.2.

When I was a junior in high school, I believed that God's will for my life was to be a physician. I later entered college in pre-med and changed to ministry my sophomore year when God called me to preach. As a high school junior, I began working in the Department of Surgery at Montgomery Baptist Medical Center in Montgomery, Alabama. The staff there provided manuals for me to study and then gave on-the-job-training to prepare me to be a surgical technician. For three years, I worked as a surgical technician and loved every minute of it. During those years, I was involved in many surgeries, but Dr. William Holding, Jr., who specialized in ear surgery, performed the one that most impressed me.

Are you familiar with the three small bones located in your middle ear? They are so small that the average medical student finds them only with great difficulty. They are the malleus, incus and stapes. Your ability to hear is dependent upon these three tiny bones functioning properly.

This most amazing surgery is called a stapedectomy. It is an operation performed on the third smallest of these bones, the stapes. The surgery is quite dramatic as the operating room is in total darkness except for the light of the microscope being used by the surgeon. The surgeon operates with instruments that have tiny tips made with remarkable precision. The procedure involves replacing the faulty stapes with an artificial one. I will always remember the thrill of the moment in that darkened room when the skilled surgeon made the connection between the artificial stapes and the other two ear bones. Dr. Holding would speak to the patient continuously. When the connection was made, the patient could hear the voice of a person speaking for the first time. I witnessed this transformation on a number of occasions, and the thrill of it was overwhelming. The patient would shout for joy and then begin weeping. The nurse would stand by to wipe away the tears. To tell you the truth, by that time, we would all be crying. It was one of the most incredible surgeries I ever witnessed.

As Christians, we should experience a natural yearning for the joy that comes in seeing people trust Christ.

Something akin to this drama occurs in the worship service when one hears the voice of God clearly, perhaps for the first time, and responds. Most often there are tears of joy from the new believer as well as the congregation. It is an experience which no church should miss. As Christians, we should experience a natural yearning for the joy that comes in seeing people trust Christ. We should want to see it so much that it hurts. The Apostle Paul had that yearning in his heart and spoke of it in 1 Corinthians 9:19-22 NASB:

"For though I am free from all men, I have made myself a slave to all, that I might win the more. And to the Jews I became as a Jew, that I might win Jews; to those who are under the Law, as under the Law, though not being myself under the Law, that I might win those who are under the Law; to those who are without law, as without law, though not being without the law of God but under the law of Christ, that I might win those who are without law. To the weak I became weak, that I might win the weak; I have become all things to all men, that I may by all means save some."

166

Was Paul trying to be all things to all people? I thought you said we should be who we are. Yes, we should be who we are, and I don't think that's what Paul was saying. I believe that Paul was doing the best he could to put himself in other people's shoes. He was attempting to see life from their perspective so that in understanding their mindset, he might be able to present the Gospel in a way that they could comprehend it. I would suggest that if we would be more like that today, we might be more successful in reaching our communities for Christ.

When we as Baptists speak to issues, we need to think about the perspective of the world. I am not saying that we should compromise our beliefs, neither do I believe that was what Paul was saying. We should communicate our position on issues and our belief in God's Word unapologetically, but wisely in such a way that the world will hear our message. We, like Paul, are free. We have trusted Christ and are saved. We don't have to try to understand the mindset of the lost person, but it surely will make us more effective communicators of the Gospel if we will. We live in an international melting pot with many cultures. Your church can declare itself a free island in the midst of an international sea, or it can make a study of the different cultures surrounding the church and seek to understand how it can most effectively communicate the Gospel of Christ to people who don't think as we think, who don't believe as we believe.

We oftentimes complain about the behavior of the world around us. To tell you the truth, the world around us is behaving in a way that is compatible with who they are. You cannot expect a lost person to act or think as you do. Lost people should not be expected to behave or think as Christians. They should be expected to behave and think as lost people. Our position should be to love people as they are, love them as people for whom Jesus died. When we see people as Jesus sees them, our perspective changes. If Jesus loved people different from you enough to give His life for them, don't you think you should love them too? In loving them, try to understand them. Understand their ways: the way they process information; the way they relate to others; the way they have been raised to practice a religion or no

Lost people should not be expected to behave or think as Christians. They should be expected to behave and think as lost people.

religion at all. Try to put yourself in their shoes as you present to them the claims of Christ. It will likely modify your approach. It will not change your message; the message never changes. It may change the way you communicate that message.

Take a look at Paul practicing what he has preached. Consider the passage in Acts 17 where Paul is in Athens. The philosophers approached Paul and said, "You are teaching some things that are strange to us. Will you please explain to us what these things mean?" Paul stood among the philosophers and identified with them. It was their custom to gather and talk about new philosophies and debate among themselves. Paul fell right in with the way they were accustomed to communicating. He honored them by telling them that he had noticed that they were a very religious people. The Athenians were probably thinking, "Yes, we are very religious. How perceptive it is of him to notice." Then Paul told them that he had been examining the objects of their worship. The

Athenians were then likely thinking, "I'm liking this fellow more and more all the time. He has taken enough interest in us to study the way we worship and our objects of worship." Then Paul told them that he had noticed their altar to the unknown god. It is this unknown god that he wanted to speak with them about on this occasion.

Do you see how Paul has put himself in their shoes, how he has tried to understand their culture and relate the Gospel to them in a way that they can understand? He also realized that before they would listen to him, he had to earn the right to be heard. This he did by being genuinely interested in them. By the time Paul got to the message of the Gospel, the philosophers were all ears. Now, as you will recall, they did not all believe in Christ through Paul's message that day, but some did. It is good for us to be reminded that we don't do the saving. We do the sowing of the Gospel seed, and God does the saving. Not everyone with whom you share the wonderful news of Christ will believe and be saved, but

It is good for us to be reminded that we don't do the saving.

some will. Wherever in the world the Gospel is being preached, people are being saved. Paul was being faithful to what God had called him to do, and so must we.

A few years ago I had the privilege of preaching a revival at a Baptist church in Seoul, South Korea. The pastor of the church was named Kim, and he was greatly beloved by his congregation. The revival was scheduled to begin on Thursday evening and conclude on Sunday morning. Each evening we had thrilling experiences of worship with people being saved in every worship service. From the time I arrived and through the weekend, Pastor Kim had been sharing with me his excitement about Sunday morning. When I asked what he had planned for the Sunday morning worship service, he said, "Oh, we are going to have a wonderful Jesus Celebration Service!" I wondered what this "Jesus Celebration Service" was all about, so I asked him to explain to me what his plan was for the service. He responded that for weeks he had been encouraging the people of his church to prepare for this great day. He wanted them to invite their lost friends, business associates, and lost family members to come to church on that day. He encouraged them not just to invite them, but also to go by, pick them up, and bring them to the church on that day so that they might hear the Gospel preached. I didn't indicate that I was concerned about his plan, but I thought to myself how we encourage our church members to do this all of the time, and people rarely bring their lost acquaintances to church.

When I asked what he had planned for the Sunday morning worship service, he said, "Oh, we are going to have a wonderful Jesus Celebration Service!"

Sunday morning arrived. As is the custom in the Korean churches, the ministers go up on the platform in advance of the service to sit quietly and pray for the worship time. The sanctuary was less than half filled when my translator, John Yi, Pastor Kim, and I went up on the platform. We began to pray silently for the time of worship. I heard the people coming in, but continued in my prayer time until Pastor Kim touched me on the arm. When I looked up, the sanctuary was filled. Every seat was taken and more people were being brought in to stand around the walls downstairs and in the balcony. Pastor Kim leaned over and said to me, "I feel like a stranger in my own church." I asked, "What do you mean, Pastor Kim?" He said, "All of these people are lost. They have never before been in any church. I have 400 members of my church who have given up their seats to their lost friends and family members, and they are in the basement praying for their salvation." I was overcome by his words. My heart filled with emotion. My eyes filled with tears. The very idea that God would ever give me the opportunity to preach to an entire church full of lost people was overwhelming. I prayed, "Dear Lord, thank You for the honor of preaching Your Gospel to this congregation of people who do not know You. How can I thank You for giving me such a privilege? I pray that You will give me the message to preach that will penetrate the hearts of these people. If You want me to preach a message different from the message I have planned, place Your words in my mouth. Please, Lord, don't let me get in the way of what You want to do in this worship service this morning. I pray that many of these people who came to this church this morning lost will go home saved."

I preached from John 3:16 that morning. I made the message as plain and simple to comprehend as I knew how. I felt the power and the presence of the Lord in that service in a unique way. When the invitation was given, the pastor asked those who wanted to give their lives to Jesus Christ to stand up. One hundred people stood up that morning saying that they wanted to give their lives to Christ. They were instructed to remain

One hundred people stood up that morning saying that they wanted to give their lives to Christ.

standing until materials could be given to them. They were taken to a counseling area where individual counselors worked with them well into the afternoon.

I left the worship service that morning thinking about all of our churches back home in the United States. As many different churches as I have preached in during the years of my ministry, I have never preached anywhere that the entire sanctuary was filled with lost people. I thought about our pastors and how they study God's Word week after week. I thought about how they pray over their sermons and deliver them passionately to congregations filled with Christians, and the lost people are on the outside of the church.

Jesus said, "Go out into the highways and hedges, and compel them to come in, that my house may be filled" (Luke 14:23 KJV).

That is exactly what the healthy church of the first century did, and the "Lord added to the church daily such as should be saved" (Acts 2:47b KJV). He did it then, and He can do it again in churches that are healthy.

PURSUE GOOD HEALTH

$\mathcal{I}$n a few days, I have an appointment with a cardiologist to get a stress test. While I have not had any indication of problems with my heart, I do have family medical history of heart trouble. It is a good idea to get a checkup just to make sure that everything is fine, and if not, to rectify the situation. Depending upon the outcome of the tests, the doctor may say that I am fine. There is nothing to be concerned about. My heart and arteries are healthy. On the other hand, he may tell me that I have blockage in my arteries in which case the severity will determine whether he prescribes medication to deal with it, performs an angioplasty, or does arterial bypass surgery. In any case, if all is not well, I would have no choice but to proceed with some form of treatment.

Whether you are the pastor, a staff minister, or a lay person in the church, you should acknowledge that a periodic checkup in the life of the church is a good idea.

Whether you are the pastor, a staff minister, or a lay person in the church, you should acknowledge that a periodic checkup in the life of the church is a good idea.

You may find that, just as you thought, your church is in excellent health. You measure up to the Biblical standard. On the other hand, through your checkup, you may discover that there are some matters that need serious attention, and some form of intervention may be necessary to correct the matter.

While not exhaustive by any means, this list of ten qualities is for the purpose of helping you check up on your church health. Since these ten qualities are Biblically-based and not author-based, you can have confidence in using them as benchmarks. It is my opinion that if a church measures up to these Scriptural standards, it is a healthy church by any analysis.

I am personally committed to each one of these qualities as being essential to church health. If you were to ask me to pick one out of the ten as the most important, it would have to be the one I listed first. Though a church may be immersed in ministry, if it fails to preach and teach the Gospel of Christ, it has failed its mission. This does not involve an evaluation of the preacher's style or whether the Sunday School teacher stands or sits to teach. This is all about content. I have been inspired by preaching that was bold and powerful, and I have been inspired by preaching that is more of a teaching style. It's not the style; it's the content that matters. The command of Christ is that we preach the Gospel. Paul's instruction to young Timothy leaves no doubt about the primacy of preaching:

"I solemnly charge you in the presence of God and of Christ Jesus, who is to judge the living and the

dead, and by His appearing and His kingdom: preach the word; be ready in season and out of season; reprove, rebuke, exhort, with great patience and instruction. For the time will come when they will not endure sound doctrine; but wanting to have their ears tickled, they will accumulate for themselves teachers in accordance to their own desires; and will turn away their ears from the truth, and will turn aside to myths. But you, be sober in all things, endure hardship, do the work of an evangelist, fulfill your ministry."
(2 Timothy 4:1-5 NASB)

Those words remind us that we are in the days that Paul cautioned Timothy about.

The fact that there are many who will not endure sound doctrine and wish to have their ears tickled rather than hear the unapologetic preaching of the Word of God should alert the church to the necessity of preaching and teaching the Gospel of Christ. Pastor, I encourage you to prepare every sermon you preach in such a way that it begins, continues, and concludes in the Word of God. Avoid the temptation to present benign messages that serve only to make everybody feel good. Preach the Gospel, and those who are saved will feel assurance; those who are lost will be convicted. Allow no one to guide your preaching but the Holy Spirit. I have many years experience as a pastor. I know that people in the church often make suggestions about what you should preach. I think it is good to be attentive to suggestions. You can always evaluate the suggestions to see if they measure favorably to your sense of God's will for your ministry. Always be courteous to people, especially when they have a stake in the success of your ministry. Then preach only what God leads you to preach. He is the One to whom you must ultimately answer.

To the laity, I would express gratitude for your faithful teaching of the Gospel of Christ in the many ministries of your church. I would encourage you in your teaching responsibilities to allow nothing to distract you from the faithful teaching of God's Word. The temptation in the classroom is to spend priceless class time discussing many things that are unrelated to the Scripture. Pray for your pastor and staff as they provide leadership for the church. You extended the invitation for them to come to your church, and they came sensing God's leadership through your call. Now it is important for you to love them, encourage them, pray for them and cheer them on when they demonstrate faithfulness to God's Word.

The other nine qualities have been listed in no particular order. My strong emphasis upon the first quality is not to say that I have any less commitment to the remaining nine. I believe that they are all necessary in order for your church to be healthy.

I am grateful that you have given me this opportunity to share with you what God has placed on my heart. May God bless you and your church as you pursue good health.